TABLE OF CONTENTS

- **3** Christmas Memories Afghan
- **13** Christmas Quilt Blocks Afghan
- **22** Christmas Dreams Afghan
- **41** Classic Christmas Blocks Afghan

General Information
- **47** Stitch Guide
- **48** Metric Conversion Charts

CHRISTMAS MEMORIES AFGHAN

Design by Rebecca J. Venton

The blocks in this afghan represent memories from Christmases past.

SKILL LEVEL
Intermediate

FINISHED MEASUREMENTS
Approximately 54 inches wide x 60 inches long

MATERIALS
- Premier Yarns Basix medium (worsted) weight acrylic yarn (7 oz/359 yds/200g per skein):
    - 3 skeins #01 white
    - 2 skeins each #95 thyme, #12 red, #94 holly and #14 burgundy
    - 1 skein each #67 toffee, #49 goldenrod and #04 black
- Size H/8/5mm crochet hook or size needed to obtain gauge
- Tapestry needle

GAUGE
13 sc = 4 inches; 15 sc rows = 4 inches

PATTERN NOTES
Weave in loose ends as work progresses.

Chain-3 at beginning of round counts as first double crochet unless otherwise stated.

Each square on a chart represents 1 single crochet. Odd rows are read right to left; even rows are read left to right *(reverse for left-handed crocheters)*.

To change color, work last yarn over with **new color** *(see illustration)* for next stitch. Work over unused color until next needed or fasten off if it will no longer be used in that block.

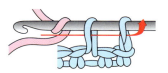

Single Crochet Color Change

SPECIAL STITCHES
Loop stitch (LS): Wrap yarn twice over index finger *(2 strands on finger)*, insert hook in indicated st, pick up lower strand and pull up a lp *(2 lps on hook)*, yo and draw working yarn through both lps. Push lp off finger.

Surface slip stitch (surface sl st): Start with slip knot on hook, insert hook in indicated sp from RS to WS, yo, pull lp to RS and through lp on hook.

AFGHAN

SANTA HAT BLOCK
Row 1: With thyme, ch 60, sc in 2nd ch from hook and in each ch across, turn. *(59 sc)*

Rows 2–7: Ch 1, sc in each st across, turn.

Row 8: Ch 1, sc in first 13 sts; with **white** *(see Pattern Notes)*, sc in next st, **LS** *(see Special Stitches)* in next 31 sts, sc in next st; with thyme, sc in next 13 sts, turn.

Row 9: Ch 1, sc in first 13 sts; with white, sc in next 33 sts; with thyme, sc in next 13 sts, turn.

Rows 10–14: Rep [rows 8 and 9] twice and then row 8 once more.

Rows 15–18: Ch 1, sc in first 13 sts; with red, sc in next 33 sts; with thyme, sc in next 13 sts, turn.

Rows 19–22: Ch 1, sc in first 14 sts; with red, sc in next 31 sts; with thyme, sc in next 14 sts, turn.

Rows 23–26: Ch 1, sc in first 15 sts; with red, sc in next 29 sts; with thyme, sc in next 15 sts, turn.

Rows 27–30: Ch 1, sc in first 16 sts; with red, sc in next 27 sts; with thyme, sc in next 16 sts, turn.

Rows 31–33: Ch 1, sc in first 17 sts; with red, sc in next 25 sts; with thyme, sc in next 17 sts, turn.

Rows 34 & 35: Ch 1, sc in first 18 sts; with red, sc in next 23 sts; with thyme, sc in next 18 sts, turn.

Row 36: Ch 1, sc in first 19 sts; with red, sc in next 21 sts; with thyme, sc in next 19 sts, turn.

Row 37: Ch 1, sc in first 20 sts; with red, sc in next 19 sts; with thyme, sc in next 20 sts, turn.

Row 38: Ch 1, sc in first 21 sts; with red, sc in next 17 sts; with thyme, sc in next 21 sts, turn.

Row 39: Ch 1, sc in first 22 sts; with red, sc in next 15 sts; with thyme, sc in next 22 sts, turn.

Row 40: Ch 1, sc in first 23 sts; with red, sc in next 13 sts; with thyme, sc in next 23 sts, turn.

Row 41: Ch 1, sc in first 25 sts; with red, sc in next 9 sts; with thyme, sc in next 25 sts, turn.

Row 42: Ch 1, sc in first 26 sts; with white, sc in next st, LS in next 5 sts, sc in next st; with thyme, sc in next 26 sts, turn.

Rows 43: Ch 1, sc in first 26 sts; with white, sc in next 7 sts; with thyme, sc in next 26 sts, turn.

Rows 44–46: Rep [rows 42 and 43] once and then row 42 once more. At end of last row, fasten off white, continue with thyme only.

Rows 47–53: Ch 1, sc in each st, across, turn. At end of row 53, fasten off.

GINGERBREAD MAN BLOCK

Row 1: With white, ch 53, sc in 2nd ch from hook and in each ch across, turn. *(52 sc)*

Rows 2–53: Ch 1, sc in each st across, turn. At end of row 53, fasten off.

GINGERBREAD MAN APPLIQUÉ

Row 1: With toffee, ch 20, sc in 2nd ch from hook and in each ch across, turn. *(19 sc)*

Row 2: Ch 1, sc in first 9 sts, **sc dec** *(see Stitch Guide)* in next 2 sts, sc in each rem st across, turn. *(18 sc)*

Row 3: Ch 1, sc in first 8 sts, sc dec in next 2 sts, sc in each rem st across, turn. *(17 sc)*

Row 4: Ch 1, sc in each st across, turn.

Row 5: Ch 1, sc dec in first 2 sts, sc in next 13 sts, sc dec in last 2 sts, turn. *(15 sc)*

Row 6: Ch 1, sc in each st across, turn.

Row 7: Ch 1, sc dec in first 2 sts, sc in next 11 sts, sc dec in last 2 sts, turn. *(13 sc)*

Rows 8 & 9: Ch 1, sc in each st across, turn.

Row 10 (arms): Ch 7, sc in 2nd ch from hook and in each rem ch and sc across, ch 7, turn. *(19 sc, 7 chs)*

Row 11: Sc in 2nd ch from hook and in each rem ch and sc across, turn. *(25 sc)*

Row 12: Ch 1, 2 sc in next st, sc in next 23 sts, 2 sc in last st, turn. *(27 sc)*

Rows 13–15: Ch 1, sc in each st across, turn.

Row 16: Ch 1, sc dec in first 2 sts, sc in next 23 sts, sc dec in last 2 sts, turn. *(25 sc)*

Row 17: Ch 1, sc in each st across, turn, fasten off.

HEAD

Row 18: Sk first 8 sts of row 17, join toffee in next st, ch 1, sc in same st and next 8 sts, turn, leaving rem sts unworked. *(9 sc)*

Row 19: Ch 1, sc in each st across, turn.

Row 20: Ch 1, 2 sc in first st, sc in next 7 sts, 2 sc in last st, turn. *(11 sc)*

Row 21: Ch 1, 2 sc in first st, sc in next 9 sts, 2 sc in last st, turn. *(13 sc)*

Row 22: Ch 1, sc each st across, turn.

Row 23: Ch 1, sc dec in first 2 sts, sc in next 9 sts, sc dec in last 2 sts, turn. *(11 sc)*

Row 24: Ch 1, sc dec in first 2 sts, sc in next 7 sts, sc dec in last 2 sts, turn. *(9 sc)*

Row 25: Ch 1, sc dec in first 2 sts, sc in next 5 sts, sc dec in last 2 sts, turn. *(7 sc)*

Row 26: Ch 1, sc dec in first 2 sts, sc in next 3 sts, sc dec in last 2 sts, turn. *(5 sc)*

Row 27: Ch 1, sc dec in first 2 sts, sc in next st, sc dec in last 2 sts, fasten off. *(3 sc)*

FIRST LEG

Row 1: Join toffee in unused lp of first st of foundation row, ch 1, sc in first 9 chs, turn, leaving rem chs unworked

Rows 2–4: Ch 1, sc in each st across, turn. *(9 sc)*

Row 5: Ch 1, sc dec in first 2 sts, sc in next 5 sts, sc dec in last 2 sts, turn. *(7 sc)*

Row 6: Ch 1, sc dec in first 2 sts, sc in next 3 sts, sc dec in last 2 sts, turn. *(5 sc)*

Row 7: Ch 1, sc dec in first 2 sts, sc in next st, sc dec in last 2 sts, fasten off. *(3 sc)*

2ND LEG

Row 1: Sk next unworked ch on foundation row, join toffee in next st, ch 1, sc in same st and next 8 chs, turn.

Rep rows 2–7 of first leg.

BORDER

Rnd 1: Join toffee in any st on outer edge of Gingerbread Man, ch 1, sc evenly around outer edge, join to first sc, fasten off.

PIPING

With 2 strands of white, embroider eyes, mouth, 3 buttons and zigzag piping at ends of both arms and legs. Sew Gingerbread Man to center of Block.

WREATH BLOCK

Row 1: With goldenrod, ch 53, sc in 2nd ch from hook and in each ch across, turn. *(52 sc)*

Rows 2–53: Ch 1, sc in each st across, turn. At end of row 53, fasten off.

WREATH APPLIQUÉ

Row 1: With holly, ch 43, sc in 2nd ch from hook and next 4 chs, 2 sc in next ch, [sc in next 5 chs, 2 sc in next ch] 6 times, turn. *(49 sc)*

Row 2: Ch 1, LS in first 6 sts, 2 sc in next st, [LS in next 6 sts, 2 sc in next st] across, turn. *(56 sts)*

Row 3: Ch 1, sc in first 7 sts, 2 sc in next st, [sc in next 7 sts, 2 sc in next st] across, turn. *(63 sc)*

Row 4: Ch 1, LS in first 8 sts, 2 sc in next st, [LS in next 8 sts, 2 sc in next st] across, turn. *(70 sts)*

Row 5: Ch 1, sc in first 9 sts, 2 sc in next st, [sc in next 9 sts, 2 sc in next st] across, turn. *(77 sc)*

Row 6: Ch 1, LS in first 10 sts, 2 sc in next st, [LS in next 10 sts, 2 sc in next st] across, turn. *(84 sc)*

Sew ends tog to form circle. Sew Wreath to center of Block.

BOW

Row 1: With red, ch 70, sl st in 2nd ch from hook and in each ch across, fasten off. *(69 sl sts)*

Tie into a bow. Sew to Wreath using photo as a guide.

MERRY BLOCK

Row 1: With burgundy, ch 111, sc in 2nd ch from hook and in each rem ch across, turn. *(110 sc)*

Rows 2–38: Following chart *(see Pattern Notes and Merry Chart)* for color changes, ch 1, sc in each st across, turn. At end of row 38, fasten off.

SANTA SUIT BLOCK

Row 1: With red, ch 33, sc in 2nd ch from hook and in each ch across, turn. *(32 sc)*

Rows 2–19: Ch 1, sc in each st across, turn.

Rows 20–26: With black, ch 1, sc in each st across, turn.

Rows 27–45: With red, ch 1, sc in each st across, turn. At end of row 45, fasten off.

BUCKLE

Row 1: With black, ch 8, sc in 2nd ch from hook and in each ch across, turn. *(7 sc)*

Rows 2–7: Ch 1, sc in each st across, turn. At end of row 7, fasten off.

COLOR KEY
☐ White
■ Burgundy

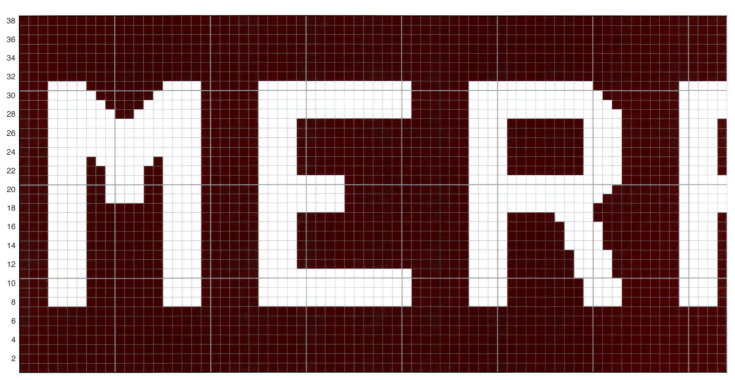

Christmas Memories Afghan
Merry Chart

BUCKLE BORDER

Rnd 1: Join goldenrod in first st of row 7, ch 1, sc in each st across, ch 3, rotate to work along side, sc in each row end, ch 3, rotate to work along foundation chs, sc in unworked lp of each foundation ch, ch 3, rotate to work along side, sc in each row end, ch 3, join to first sc. Fasten off.

Sew to center of Block.

PRESENTS BLOCK

Row 1: With holly, ch 79, sc in 2nd ch from hook and in each rem ch across, turn. *(78 sc)*

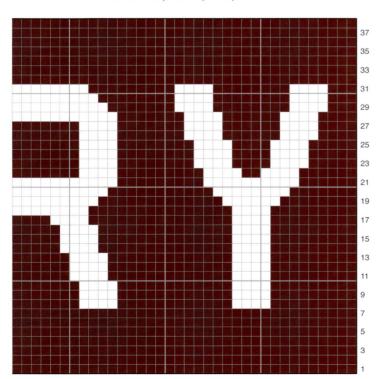

Rows 2–7: Ch 1, sc in each st across, turn.

Row 8: Ch 1, sc in first 7 sts; with red, sc in next 7 sts; with goldenrod, sc in next 7 sts; with red, sc in next 7 sts; with holly, sc in next 8 sts; with red, sc in next 14 sts; with goldenrod, sc in next 7 sts; with red, sc in next 14 sts; with holly, sc in rem sts, turn.

Row 9: Ch 1, sc in first 7 sts; with red, sc in next 14 sts; with goldenrod, sc in next 7 sts; with red, sc in next 14 sts; with holly, sc in next 8 sts; with red, sc in next 7 sts; with goldenrod, sc in next 7 sts; with red, sc in next 7 sts; with holly, sc in rem sts, turn.

Rows 10–22: Rep [rows 8 and 9] 6 times, then row 8 once more.

Row 23: Ch 1, sc in first 7 sts; with red, sc in next 14 sts; with goldenrod, sc in next 7 sts; with red, sc in next 14 sts; with holly, sc in rem sts, turn.

Row 24: Ch 1, sc in first 36 sts; with red, sc in next 14 sts; with goldenrod, sc in next 7 sts; with red, sc in next 14 sts; with holly, sc in rem sts, turn.

Rows 25–30: Rep rows 23 and 24. At end of last row, fasten off red and goldenrod. Continue with holly.

Rows 31–45: Ch 1, sc in each st across, turn. At end of row 45, fasten off.

BOW

Make 2 with goldenrod as for Wreath Block.
Tie into a bow. Sew to top of Presents.

SNOWMAN BLOCK

Row 1: With white, ch 53, sc in 2nd ch from hook and in each ch across, turn. *(52 sc)*

Rows 2–38: Ch 1, sc in each st across, turn.

Rows 39–46: Ch 1, sc in first 14 sts; with red, sc in next 24 sts; with white, sc in last 14 sts, turn. After row 46, fasten off red.

Rows 47–83: Ch 1, sc in each st across, turn. At end of row 83, fasten off.

COAL
Make 10.

Rnd 1: With black, form a **slip ring** *(see illustration)*, ch 1, 7 sc in ring, join in first st. *(7 sc)*

Rnd 2: Ch 1, 2 sc in each st around, join in first st. Fasten off. *(14 sc)*

Sew to Block using 2 pieces of Coal for eyes, 5 for mouth and 3 for buttons.

4" end

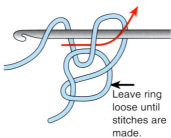
Leave ring loose until stitches are made.

Slip Ring

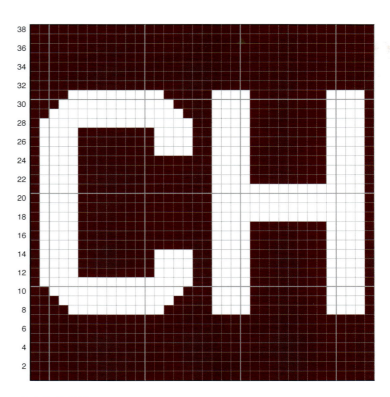

CARROT

Row 1: With red, ch 8, sc in 2nd ch from hook and in each ch across, turn. *(7 sc)*

Rows 2 & 3: Ch 1, sc in each st across, turn.

Row 4: Ch 1, sc dec in first 2 sts, sc in next 3 sts, sc dec in last 2 sts, turn. *(5 sc)*

Rows 5–7: Ch 1, sc in each st across, turn.

Row 8: Ch 1, sc dec in first 2 sts, sc in next st, sc dec in last 2 sts, turn. *(3 sc)*

Rows 9–11: Ch 1, sc in each st across, turn.

Row 12: Ch 1, sc dec in all 3 sts, turn. *(1 sc)*

Row 13: Ch 1, sc in st. Fasten off.

Sew Carrot between eyes and mouth.

CHRISTMAS BLOCK

Row 1: With burgundy, ch 163, sc in 2nd ch from hook and in each rem ch across, turn. *(162 sc)*

Rows 2–38: Following chart *(see Pattern Notes and Christmas Chart)* for color changes, ch 1, sc in each st across, turn. At end of row 38, fasten off.

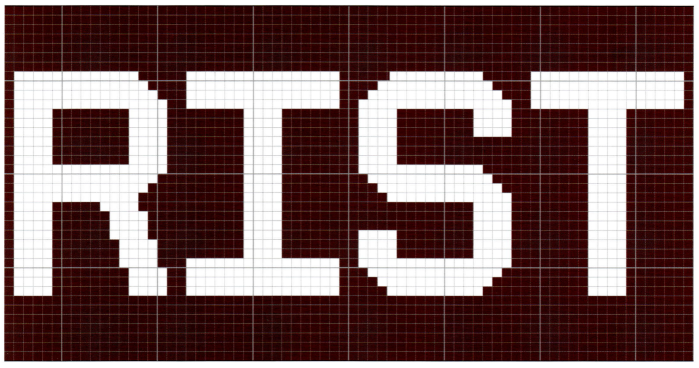

Christmas Memories Afghan
Christmas Chart

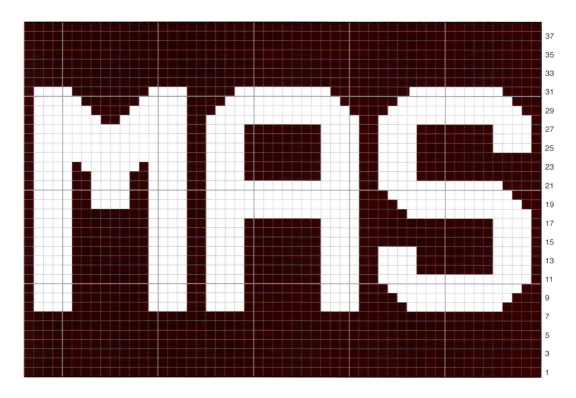

STAR BLOCK

Row 1: With white, ch 33, sc in 2nd ch from hook and in each ch across, turn. *(32 sc)*

Rows 2–38: Ch 1, sc in each st across, turn. At end of row 38, fasten off.

STAR APPLIQUÉ
Rnd 1: With goldenrod, form a slip ring, ch 1, 5 sc in ring, join in beg sc. *(5 sc)*

Rnd 2: Ch 1, 2 sc in each st around, join in beg sc. *(10 sc)*

Rnd 3: Ch 1, 2 sc in each st around, join in beg sc. *(20 sc)*

Rnd 4: Ch 1, sc in first st, 2 sc in next st, [sc in next st, 2 sc in next st] around, join in beg sc. *(30 sc)*

STAR POINT
Row 5: Ch 1, sc in first 6 sts, turn, leaving rem sts unworked. *(6 sc)*

Row 6: Ch 1, sc dec in first 2 sts, sc in next 2 sts, sc dec in last 2 sts, turn. *(4 sc)*

Row 7: Ch 1, sc in each st across, turn.

Row 8: Ch 1, sc dec in first 2 sts, sc dec in last 2 sts, turn. *(2 sc)*

Row 9: Ch 1, sc in each st across, turn.

Row 10: Ch 1, sc dec in 2 sts, turn. *(1 sc)*

Row 11: Ch 1, sc in st, fasten off.

[Join yarn in next unworked st of rnd 4. Rep Star Point rows 5–11] 5 times.

Sew to center of Block.

MITTENS BLOCK

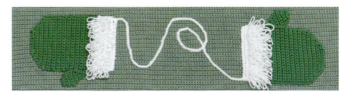

Row 1: With thyme, ch 131, sc in 2nd ch from hook and in each ch across, turn. *(130 sc)*

Rows 2–39: Ch 1, sc in each st across, turn. At end of row 39, fasten off.

MITTEN APPLIQUÉ
Make 2.

Row 1: With white, ch 21, sc in 2nd ch from hook and in each rem ch across, turn. *(20 sc)*

Row 2: Ch 1, LS in each st across, turn.

Row 3: Ch 1, sc in each st across, turn.

Rows 4–8: Rep [rows 2 and 3] twice and row 2 once more. At end of last row, fasten off.

Rows 9–30: With holly, ch 1, sc in each st across, turn.

Row 31: Ch 1, sc dec in first 2 sts, sc in next 16 sts, sc dec in last 2 sts, turn. *(18 sc)*

Row 32: Ch 1, sc dec in first 2 sts, sc in next 14 sts, sc dec in last 2 sts, turn. *(16 sc)*

Row 33: Ch 1, sc dec in first 2 sts, sc in next 12 sts, sc dec in last 2 sts, turn. *(14 sc)*

Row 34: Ch 1, sc dec in first 2 sts, sc in next 10 sts, sc dec in last 2 sts, turn. *(12 sc)*

Row 35: Ch 1, sc dec in first 2 sts, sc in next 8 sts, sc dec in last 2 sts, turn. *(10 sc)*

Row 36: Ch 1, sc dec in first 2 sts, sc in next 6 sts, sc dec in last 2 sts, fasten off. *(8 sc)*

THUMB
Make 2.

Row 1: With holly, ch 2, sc in 2nd ch from hook, turn. *(1 sc)*

Row 2: Ch 1, 2 sc in st, turn. *(2 sc)*

Row 3: Ch 1, sc in each st across, turn.

Row 4: Ch 1, 2 sc in each st across, turn. *(4 sc)*

Row 5: Ch 1, sc in each st across, turn.

Row 6: Ch 1, 2 sc in first st, sc in next 2 sts, 2 sc in last st, turn. *(6 sc)*

Rows 7 & 8: Ch 1, sc in each st across, turn.

Row 9: Ch 1, sc dec in first 2 sts, sc in next 2 sts, sc dec in last 2 sts, turn. *(4 sc)*

Row 10: Ch 1, sc in each st across, turn.

Row 11: Ch 1, sc dec in first 2 sts, sc dec in last 2 sts, fasten off. *(2 sc)*

Sew rows 1–7 of Thumb to left side of rows 11–17 of each Mitten.

Sew Mittens to opposite ends of Block.

With white, **surface sl st** *(see Special Stitches)* from 1 mitten to other using photo as a guide.

ASSEMBLY
Block individual blocks before assembly. Following Assembly Diagram, sew Blocks tog using whipstitch.

BORDER
Rnd 1: Join red in first sc at top right corner of blanket, ch 1, sc in each st across, ch 3, rotate to work down side, *sc in each row end *(if needed sk every 5th row to keep border even)*, ch 3, sc in each st across bottom of afghan, ch 3, rotate to work up side, rep between * once, ch 3, join in beg sc.

Rnd 2: Ch 3 *(see Pattern Notes)*, dc in each st around, working (2 dc, ch 2, 2 dc) in each ch-3 corner sp, join in top of beg ch-3. Fasten off.

Rnd 3: Join burgundy in any ch-2 corner sp, ch 3, (dc, ch 2, 2 dc) in same corner sp, dc in each st around, working (2 dc, ch 2, 2 dc) in each corner ch-2 sp, join in top of beg ch-3, sl st in next dc and next ch-2 sp.

Rnd 4: Ch 3, (dc, ch 2, 2 dc) in same corner sp, dc in each st around, working (2 dc, ch 2, 2 dc) in each ch-2 corner sp, join in top of beg ch-3, fasten off. ●

Christmas Memories Afghan
Block Chart

CHRISTMAS QUILT BLOCKS AFGHAN

Design by Kathleen Berlew

Tapestry crochet is used to create these beautiful tile blocks featuring traditional Christmas colors. Fun tassels are added to each corner for an elegant touch.

SKILL LEVEL
Intermediate

FINISHED MEASUREMENT
60 inches square

MATERIALS
- Premier Yarns Anti-Pilling Everyday Worsted medium (worsted) weight acrylic yarn (3½ oz/180 yds/100g per skein):
    - 7 skeins each #100-07 really red and #100-01 snow white
    - 4 skeins #100-82 green apple
- Size H/8/5mm crochet hook or size needed to obtain gauge
- Tapestry needle
- Stitch marker

GAUGE
In tapestry dc: 13½ sts = 4 inches; 7 rows = 4 inches

PATTERN NOTES
Blanket is composed of 16 blocks, 4 each worked from 4 different charts. The finished blocks are sewn together and finished with a single crochet border.

Each block is worked in joined rounds from the center out, with each color on the Chart Key indicating the stitches used.

To change color in indicated stitch, work last yarn over with new color.

Carry unused yarn color along top of stitches of previous row, working over the strand not in use.

Take care to maintain even tension so carried yarn doesn't affect gauge.

Chain-3 at beginning of round counts as first double crochet unless otherwise stated.

Join with slip stitch as indicated unless otherwise stated.

Weave in loose ends as work progresses.

SPECIAL STITCH

Single crochet join (sc join): Place slip knot on hook, insert hook in indicated st, yo, pull up a lp, yo, draw through both lps on hook.

AFGHAN

BLOCK A
Make 4.

Rnd 1 (RS): With green apple, ch 4, **join** *(see Pattern Notes)* in 4th ch from hook to form a ring, **ch 3** *(see Pattern Notes)*, dc in ring, [ch 2, 3 dc in ring] 3 times, ch 2, dc in ring, join in top of beg ch-3. *(12 dc, 4 ch-2 sps)*

Rnd 2: Ch 3, dc in next dc, ***change color** (see Stitch Guide and Pattern Notes)* to snow white, **working over green apple** *(see Pattern Notes)*, (2 dc, ch 2, 2 dc) in next ch-2 sp**, change to green apple, working over snow white, dc in next 3 dc, rep from * around, ending last rep at **, change to green apple, working over snow white, dc in next dc, join in top of beg ch-3. *(28 dc, 4 ch-2 sps)*

Rnds 3–12: Referring to **Chart** *(see Block A Chart and Pattern Notes)*, ch 3, dc in each dc around, working (2 dc, ch 2, 2 dc) in each ch-2 sp, changing color as indicated and working over color not in use, join in top of beg ch-3 at end of each rnd. Fasten off each color when it is no longer needed, fasten off last color at end of rnd 12. *(204 dc)*

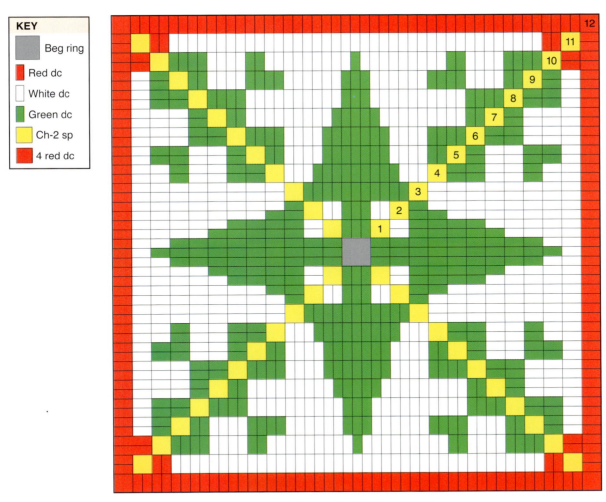

Christmas Quilt Blocks Afghan
Block A Chart

BLOCK B
Make 4.

Rnd 1 (RS): With green apple, ch 4, join in 4th ch from hook to form a ring, ch 3, dc in ring, [ch 2, 3 dc in ring] 3 times, ch 2, dc in ring, change to snow white, join in top of beg ch-3. *(12 dc, 4 ch-2 sps)*

Rnd 2: With snow white, ch 3, *change to green apple, working over snow white, dc in next dc, (2 dc, ch 2, 2 dc) in next ch-2 sp, dc in next dc, change to snow white**, working over green apple, dc in next dc, rep from * around, ending last rep at **, join in top of beg ch-3. *(28 dc, 4 ch-2 sps)*

Rnds 3–12: Work as rnds 3–12 of Block A, referring to **Chart** *(see Block B Chart). (204 dc)*

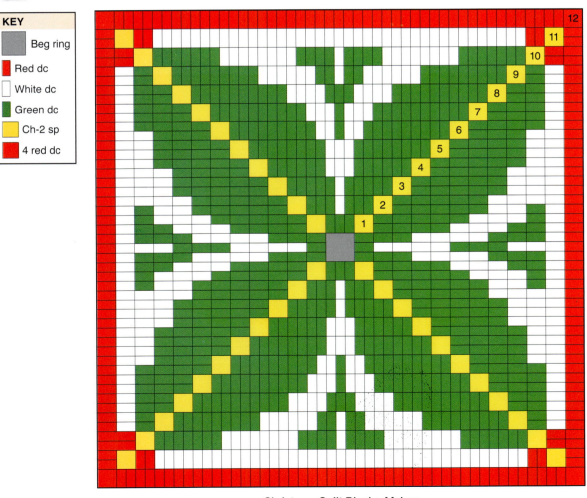

Christmas Quilt Blocks Afghan
Block B Chart

BLOCK C
Make 4.

Rnd 1 (RS): With really red, ch 4, join in 4th ch from hook to form a ring, ch 3, dc in ring, [ch 2, 3 dc in ring] 3 times, ch 2, dc in ring, change to snow white, join in top of beg ch-3. *(12 dc, 4 ch-2 sps)*

Rnd 2: With snow white, ch 3, working over really red, dc in next dc, *change to really red, working over snow white, (2 dc, ch 2, 2 dc) in next ch-2 sp, change to snow white**, working over really red, dc in next 3 dc, rep from * around, ending last rep at **, working over snow white, dc in next dc, join in top of beg ch-3. *(28 dc, 4 ch-2 sps)*

Rnds 3–12: Work as rnds 3–12 of Block A, referring to **Chart** *(see Block C Chart)*. *(204 dc)*

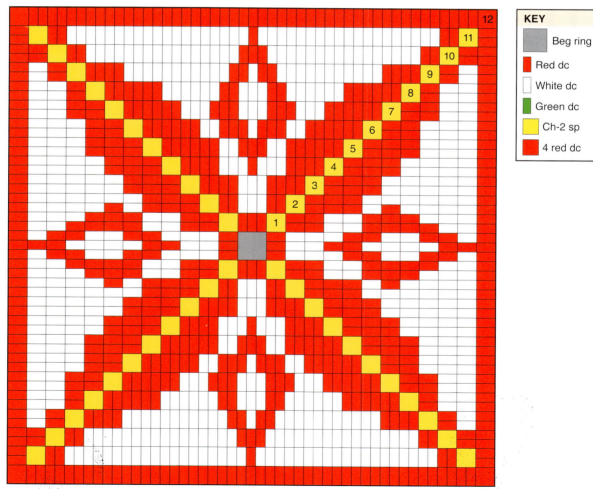

Christmas Quilt Blocks Afghan
Block C Chart

BLOCK D
Make 4.

Rnds 1–12: Work as rnds 1–12 of Block C, referring to **Chart** (see Block D Chart). (204 dc)

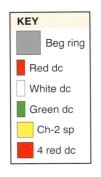

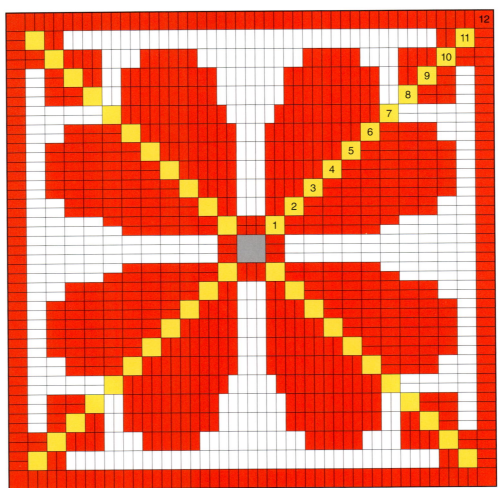

Christmas Quilt Blocks Afghan
Block D Chart

ASSEMBLY

Steam-block each block to 15 inches by 15 inches. Arrange blocks as shown in Assembly Diagram and sew tog.

BORDER

Rnd 1 (RS): Sc join *(see Special Stitch)* really red in any st, *sc in each st across** to 2 sts before next ch-2 sp, sc in next st, 2 sc in next st, ch 2, 2 sc in next st, sc in next st, rep from * around, ending last rep at **, join in beg sc, fasten off.

TASSEL

Make 4.

Cut 75 12-inch strands of snow white. Tie a 14-inch doubled strand of really red tightly around center of snow white strand bundle, leaving long tails. Fold tassel strands in half and tie another 14-inch strand of snow white around folded bundle about ¾ inch from top. With tapestry needle, pull snow white tails to center of tassel. Set aside.

Christmas Quilt Blocks Afghan
Assembly Diagram

CAP

Rnd 1: With really red, make a **slip ring** *(see illustration)*, ch 1, 6 sc in ring, pull end to tighten ring. *(6 sc)*

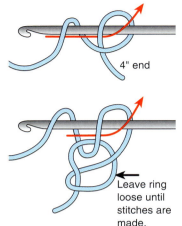

Slip Ring

Rnd 2: 2 sc in each sc around, place stitch marker in first st of rnd. *(12 sc)*

Rnds 3–5: Sc in each st around, moving marker to first st of each rnd.

Rnd 6: [**Sc dec** *(see Stitch Guide)* over next 2 sts] 6 times, join in first sc, fasten off. *(6 sc)*

Rnd 7: Sc join green apple in any st of rnd 6, 2 sc in each st around, join in beg sc, fasten off, leaving a long tail.

Designer's Tip

If tassels are crimped, use a steamer to smooth and straighten them before tying and trimming.

TASSEL ASSEMBLY

With tapestry needle, draw 4 really red tie strands of tassel through slip ring to outside top of cap. Pull cap down over ball portion of tassel, like a hat, so green apple rnd conceals snow white tie strand. With tapestry needle, weave green apple tail under bases of green apple sts around cap, cinch strand to secure cap in place. Trim tail and weave in end.

MACRAMÉ TIES

For each tassel, cut 12 6-inch strands of snow white.

Using outer layer of strands on tassel, divide 48 strands into 6 groups of 8 strands each. Wrap a strand of yarn tightly around 8 strands approximately 1 inch from top, tie a firm knot in back and cut strands close to knot. Rep on all 6 strand groups to complete first tier.

Rep for 2nd tier, using 4 strands from each of 2 groups of strands and tying a strand around new group of 8 strands as before, approximately 1 inch below first tier of knots.

FINISHING

Trim tassel ends even.

Use really red tails to attach 1 tassel in each corner of blanket. ●

CHRISTMAS DREAMS AFGHAN

Design by Lisa Gentry

Tapestry crochet is used to create stripes of traditional Christmas images. Keep sweet memories alive as you stitch this beautiful afghan.

SKILL LEVEL
Intermediate

FINISHED MEASUREMENTS
43 inches wide x 46 inches long (blocked)

MATERIALS
- Premier Yarns Anti-Pilling Everyday Worsted medium (worsted) weight acrylic yarn (3½ oz/165 yds/100g per skein):
    - 3 skeins each #100-07 really red (A) and #100-01 snow white (B)
    - 2 skeins each #100-87 meadow (C), #100-77 fern green (D), #100-82 green apple (F) and #100-85 azalea (G)
    - 1 skein #100-92 rosewood (E)
- Size H/8/5mm crochet hook or size needed to obtain gauge
- Size I/9/5.5mm crochet hook
- Removable stitch markers: 4
- Tapestry needle

GAUGE
With smaller hook: 16 sc = 4 inches; 17 sc rows = 4 inches

To save time, take time to check gauge.

PATTERN NOTES
To change color in indicated stitch, work last yarn over with **new color** (see illustration on page 24).

For each stripe, carry color not in use along top of previous row, working over the yarn until it is needed.

Fasten off colors when each stripe is completed, or color(s) may be carried up the edge of the work until needed.

Refer to charts as needed.

Weave in loose ends as work progresses.

Chain-1 at beginning of row does not count as a stitch.

Chain-3 at beginning of row or round counts as first double crochet unless otherwise stated.

Join with slip stitch as indicated unless otherwise stated.

Move stitch markers up as work progresses, keeping marker in center stitch of corner group just made.

AFGHAN
Row 1 (WS): With A and larger hook, ch 160, sc in 2nd ch and in each ch across, **change color** (see Pattern Notes) to B in last st, turn. (159 sc)

Row 2 (RS): Ch 1 (see Pattern Notes), sc in each sc across, change color to A, turn, **fasten off** (see Pattern Notes) B.

Row 3: Ch 1, sc in each sc across, change color to C, turn, fasten off A.

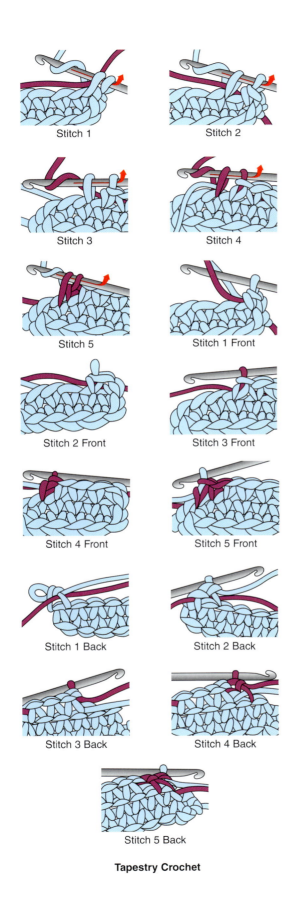

Tapestry Crochet

STRIPE 1: TREES

Row 1 (RS): With RS facing, ch 1, sc in each st across, turn.

Row 2: Change to smaller hook, **working over color not in use** (see Pattern Notes), with C, sc in first 3 sts; [with D, sc in next st; with C, sc in next 7 sts] 19 times; with D, sc in next st; with C, sc in next 3 sts, turn.

Row 3: Ch 1, with C, sc in first 3 sts; [with D, sc in next st; with C, sc in next 7 sts] 19 times; with D, sc in next st; with C, sc in next 3 sts, turn.

Row 4: Ch 1, [with D, sc in first/next 7 sts; with C, sc in next st] 19 times; with D, sc in next 7 sts, turn.

Rows 5 & 6: Ch 1, with C, sc in first st; [with D, sc in next 5 sts; with C, sc in next 3 sts] 19 times; with D, sc in next 5 sts; with C, sc in next st, turn.

Rows 7 & 8: Ch 1, with C, sc in first 2 sts; [with D, sc in next 3 sts; with C, sc in next 5 sts] 19 times; with D, sc in next 3 sts; with C, sc in next 2 sts, turn.

Rows 9 & 10: Ch 1, with C, sc in first 3 sts; [with D, sc in next st; with C, sc in next 7 sts] 19 times; with D, sc in next st; with C, sc in next 3 sts, turn, fasten off D.

Row 11: Change to larger hook, ch 1, sc in each st across, turn, fasten off C.

STRIPE 2: CANDY CANES

Row 1 (RS): With larger hook and RS facing, **join** (see Pattern Notes) B in first st, ch 1, sc in each st across, turn.

Row 2: Ch 1, sc in each st across, turn.

Row 3: Change to smaller hook, working over color not in use, ch 1, [with B, sc in first/next 3 sts; with A, sc in next st] 39 times; with B, sc in next 3 sts, turn.

Row 4: Ch 1, with B, sc in first 2 sts; [with A, sc in next st; with B, sc in next 3 sts] 39 times; with A, sc in next st, turn.

Row 5: Ch 1; with B, sc in first st; [with A, sc in next st; with B, sc in next 3 sts] 39 times; with A, sc in next st; with B, sc in next st, turn.

Row 6: Ch 1, [with A, sc in first/next st; with B, sc in next 3 sts] 39 times; with A, sc in next st; with B, sc in next 2 sts, turn, fasten off A.

Rows 7 & 8: Change to larger hook, with B, ch 1, sc in each st across, turn, fasten off B at end of row 8.

STRIPE 3: GIFTS

Row 1 (RS): With larger hook and RS facing, join E in first st, ch 1, sc in each st across, turn.

Row 2: Ch 1, sc in each st across, turn.

Row 3: Change to smaller hook, working over color not in use, ch 1, [with E, sc in first/next 5 sts; with G, sc in next 4 sts; with E, sc in next st; with G, sc in next 4 sts] 11 times; with E, sc in next 5 sts, turn.

Rows 4 & 5: Ch 1, [with E, sc in first/next 5 sts; with G, sc in next 4 sts; with E, sc in next st; with G, sc in next 4 sts] 11 times; with E, sc in next 5 sts, turn.

Row 6: Working over G for entire row, ch 1, with E, sc in each st across, turn.

Rows 7 & 8: Ch 1, [with E, sc in first/next 5 sts; with G, sc in next 4 sts; with E, sc in next st; with G, sc in next 4 sts] 11 times; with E, sc in next 5 sts, turn.

Row 9: Ch 1, with E, sc in first 9 sts; [with G, sc in next st; with E, sc in next 13 sts] 10 times; with G, sc in next st; with E, sc in next 9 sts, turn.

Row 10: Ch 1, with E, sc in first 7 sts; [with G, sc in next 2 sts; with E, sc in next st; with G, sc in next 2 sts; with E, sc in next 9 sts] 10 times; with G, sc in next 2 sts; with E, sc in next st; with G, sc in next 2 sts; with E, sc in next 7 sts, turn.

Row 11: Ch 1, with E, sc in first 6 sts; [with G, sc in next 3 sts; with E, sc in next st; with G, sc in next 3 sts; with E, sc in next 7 sts] 10 times; with G, sc in next 3 sts; with E, sc in next st; with G, sc in next 3 sts; with E, sc in next 6 sts, turn.

Row 12: Ch 1, with E, sc in first 6 sts; [with G, sc in next 2 sts; with E, sc in next 3 sts; with G, sc in next 2 sts; with E, sc in next 7 sts] 10 times; with G, sc in next 2 sts; with E, sc in next 3 sts; with G, sc in next 2 sts; with E, sc in next 6 sts, turn, fasten off G.

Rows 13 & 14: Change to larger hook, with E, ch 1, sc in each st across, turn, fasten off E at end of row 14.

STRIPE 4: SNOWFLAKES

Row 1 (RS): With larger hook and RS facing, join F in first st, ch 1, sc in each st across, turn.

Row 2: Ch 1, sc in each st across, turn.

Rows 3 & 4: With B, ch 1, sc in each st across, turn.

Row 5: Change to smaller hook, working over color not in use, with B, sc in first 4 sts; [with F, sc in next st; with B, sc in next 2 sts] 2 times; [with F, sc in next st; with B, sc in next 9 sts; with F, sc in next st; with B, sc in next 2 sts; with F, sc in next st; with B, sc in next 2 sts] 9 times; with F, sc in next st; with B, sc in next 4 sts, turn.

Row 6: Ch 1, with B, sc in first 4 sts; [with F, sc in next 2 sts; with B, sc in next 3 sts; with F, sc in next 2 sts; with B, sc in next 9 sts] 9 times; with F, sc in next 2 sts; with B, sc in next 3 sts; with F, sc in next 2 sts; with B, sc in next 4 sts, turn.

Rows 7 & 8: Ch 1, with B, sc in first 4 sts; [with F, sc in next 3 sts; with B, sc in next st; with F, sc in next 3 sts; with B, sc in next 9 sts] 9 times; with F, sc in next 3 sts; with B, sc in next st; with F, sc in next 3 sts; with B, sc in next 4 sts, turn.

Row 9: Ch 1, [with F, sc in first/next 4 sts; with B, sc in next st; with F, sc in next 2 sts; with B, sc in next st; with F, sc in next 2 sts; with B, sc in next st; with F, sc in next 4 sts; with B, sc in next st] 9 times; with F, sc in next 4 sts; [with B, sc in next st; with F, sc in next 2 sts] 2 times; with B, sc in next st; with F, sc in next 4 sts, turn.

Row 10: Ch 1, with B, sc in first st; [with F, sc in next 4 sts; with B, sc in next st; with F, sc in next st; with B, sc in next st; with F, sc in next st; with B, sc in next st; with F, sc in next 4 sts; with B, sc in next 3 sts] 9 times; with F, sc in next 4 sts; [with B, sc in next st; with F, sc in next st] 2 times; with B, sc in next st; with F, sc in next 4 sts; with B, sc in next st, turn.

Row 11: Ch 1, with B, sc in first 2 sts; [with F, sc in next 4 sts; with B, sc in next st; with F, sc in next st; with B, sc in next st; with F, sc in next 4 sts; with B, sc in next 5 sts] 9 times; with F, sc in next 4 sts; with B, sc in next st; with F, sc in next st; with B, sc in next st; with F, sc in next 4 sts; with B, sc in next 2 sts, turn.

Row 12: Ch 1, [with B, sc in first/next 6 sts; with F, sc in next st; with B, sc in next st; with F, sc in next st; with B, sc in next 6 sts; with F, sc in next st] 9 times; with B, sc in next 6 sts; with F, sc in next st; with B, sc in next st; with F, sc in next st; with B, sc in next 6 sts, turn.

Row 13: Ch 1, with B, sc in first 2 sts; [with F, sc in next 4 sts; with B, sc in next st; with F, sc in next st; with B, sc in next st; with F, sc in next 4 sts; with B, sc in next 5 sts] 9 times; with F, sc in next 4 sts; with B, sc in next st; with F, sc in next st; with B, sc in next st; with F, sc in next 4 sts; with B, sc in next 2 sts, turn.

Row 14: Ch 1, with B, sc in first st; [with F, sc in next 4 sts; with B, sc in next st; with F, sc in next st; with B, sc in next st; with F, sc in next st; with B, sc in next st; with F, sc in next 4 sts; with B, sc in next 3 sts] 9 times; with F, sc in next 4 sts; [with B, sc in next st; with F, sc in next st] 2 times; with B, sc in next st; with F, sc in next 4 sts; with B, sc in next st, turn.

Row 15: Ch 1, [with F, sc in first/next 4 sts; with B, sc in next st; with F, sc in next 2 sts; with B, sc in next st; with F, sc in next 2 sts; with B, sc in next st; with F, sc in next 4 sts; with B, sc in next st] 9 times; with F, sc in next 4 sts; [with B, sc in next st; with F, sc in next 2 sts] 2 times; with B, sc in next st; with F, sc in next 4 sts, turn.

Rows 16 & 17: Ch 1, with B, sc in first 4 sts; [with F, sc in next 3 sts; with B, sc in next st; with F, sc in next 3 sts; with B, sc in next 9 sts] 9 times; with F, sc in next 3 sts; with B, sc in next st; with F, sc in next 3 sts; with B, sc in next 4 sts, turn.

Row 18: Ch 1, with B, sc in first 4 sts; [with F, sc in next 2 sts; with B, sc in next 3 sts; with F, sc in next 2 sts; with B, sc in next 9 sts] 9 times; with F, sc in next 2 sts; with B, sc in next 3 sts; with F, sc in next 2 sts; with B, sc in next 4 sts, turn.

Row 19: Ch 1, with B, sc in first 4 sts; [with F, sc in next st; with B, sc in next 2 sts] 2 times; [with F, sc in next st; with B, sc in next 9 sts; with F, sc in next st; with B, sc in next 2 sts; with F, sc in next st; with B, sc in next 2 sts] 9 times; with B, sc in next 4 sts, turn.

Row 20: Change to larger hook, drop F to back of work, with B, ch 1, sc in each st across, turn.

Row 21: Ch 1, sc in each st across, turn, fasten off B.

Rows 22 & 23: With F, ch 1, sc in each st across, turn, fasten off F at end of row 23.

STRIPE 5: ORNAMENTS

Row 1 (RS): With larger hook and RS facing, join G in first st, ch 1, sc in each st across.

Row 2: Ch 1, sc in each st across, turn.

Rows 3 & 4: With A, ch 1, sc in each st across, turn.

Row 5: Change to smaller hook, working over color not in use, ch 1, with A, sc in first 3 sts; [with B, sc in next 3 sts; with A, sc in next 7 sts] 15 times; with B, sc in next 3 sts; with A, sc in next 3 sts, turn.

Row 6: Ch 1, with A, sc in first 2 sts; [with B, sc in next 5 sts; with A, sc in next 5 sts] 15 times; with B, sc in next 5 sts; with A, sc in next 2 sts, turn.

Row 7: Ch 1, with A, sc in first st; [with B, sc in next 7 sts; with A, sc in next 3 sts] 15 times; with B, sc in next 7 sts; with A, sc in next st, turn.

Row 8: Ch 1, with A, sc in first st; [with G, sc in next 7 sts; with A, sc in next 3 sts] 15 times; with G, sc in next 7 sts; with A, sc in next st, turn.

Row 9: Ch 1, with A, sc in first st; [with B, sc in next 7 sts; with A, sc in next 3 sts] 15 times; with B, sc in next 7 sts; with A, sc in next st, turn.

Row 10: Ch 1, with A, sc in first 2 sts; [with B, sc in next 5 sts; with A, sc in next 5 sts] 15 times; with B, sc in next 5 sts; with A, sc in next 2 sts, turn.

Row 11: Ch 1, with A, sc in first 3 sts; [with B, sc in next 3 sts; with A, sc in next 7 sts] 15 times; with B, sc in next 3 sts; with A, sc in next 3 sts, turn, fasten off B.

Row 12: Ch 1, with A, sc in first 4 sts; [with G, sc in next st; with A, sc in next 9 sts] 15 times; with G, sc in next st; with A, sc in next 4 sts, turn.

Row 13: Change to larger hook, drop G to back of work, with A, ch 1, sc in each st across, turn.

Row 14: Ch 1, sc in each st across, turn, fasten off A.

Rows 15 & 16: With G, ch 1, sc in each st across, turn, fasten off G at end of row 16.

STRIPE 6: REINDEER

Row 1 (RS): With larger hook and RS facing, join D in first st, ch 1, sc in each st across, turn.

Row 2: Ch 1, sc in each st across, turn.

Rows 3 & 4: With C, ch 1, sc in each st across, turn.

Row 5: Change to smaller hook, working over color not in use, with C, ch 1, sc in first 5 sts; [with D, sc in next st; with C, sc in next st; with D, sc in next st; with C, sc in next 3 sts; with D, sc in next st; with C, sc in next st; with D, sc in next st; with C, sc in next 7 sts] 9 times; with D, sc in next st; with C, sc in next st; with D, sc in next st; with C, sc in next 3 sts; [with D, sc in next st; with C, sc in next st] 2 times, turn.

Rows 6–8: Ch 1, with C, sc in first 5 sts; [with D, sc in next st; with C, sc in next st; with D, sc in next st; with C, sc in next 3 sts; with D, sc in next st; with C, sc in next st; with D, sc in next st; with C, sc in next 7 sts] 9 times; with D, sc in next st; with C, sc in next st; with D, sc in next st; with C, sc in next 3 sts; [with D, sc in next st; with C, sc in next st] 2 times, turn.

Rows 9–11: Ch 1, with C, sc in first 5 sts; [with D, sc in next 9 sts; with C, sc in next 7 sts] 9 times; with D, sc in next 9 sts; with C, sc in next st, turn.

Row 12: Ch 1, with C, sc in first 4 sts; [with D, sc in next 9 sts; with C, sc in next st; with D, sc in next st; with C, sc in next 5 sts] 9 times; with D, sc in next 9 sts; with C, sc in next st, turn.

Row 13: Ch 1, with C, sc in first st; [with D, sc in next 6 sts; with C, sc in next 7 sts; with D, sc in next st; with C, sc in next 2 sts] 9 times; with D, sc in next 6 sts; with C, sc in next 7 sts; with D, sc in next st, turn.

Row 14: Ch 1, with C, sc in first st; [with D, sc in next 6 sts; with C, sc in next 10 sts] 9 times; with D, sc in next 6 sts; with C, sc in next 8 sts, turn.

Row 15: Ch 1, with C, sc in first 3 sts; [with D, sc in next 2 sts; with C, sc in next st; with D, sc in next 2 sts; with C, sc in next 11 sts] 9 times; with D, sc in next 2 sts; with C, sc in next st; with D, sc in next 2 sts; with C, sc in next 7 sts, turn.

Row 16: Ch 1, with C, sc in first 4 sts; [with D, sc in next 3 sts; with C, sc in next 13 sts] 9 times; with D, sc in next 3 sts; with C, sc in next 8 sts, turn.

Row 17: Ch 1, [with C, sc in first/next 3 sts; with D, sc in next st] 2 times; [with C, sc in next 11 sts; with D, sc in next st; with C, sc in next 3 sts; with D, sc in next st] 9 times; with C, sc in next 7 sts, turn.

Row 18: Ch 1, with C, sc in first 2 sts; [with D, sc in next 2 sts; with C, sc in next 3 sts; with D, sc in next 2 sts; with C, sc in next 9 sts] 9 times; with D, sc in next 2 sts; with C, sc in next 3 sts; with D, sc in next 2 sts; with C, sc in next 6 sts, turn.

Row 19: Ch 1, [with D, sc in first/next 2 sts; with C, sc in next st; with D, sc in next st; with C, sc in next 3 sts; with D, sc in next st; with C, sc in next st; with D, sc in next 2 sts; with C, sc in next 5 sts] 9 times; with D, sc in next 2 sts; with C, sc in next st; with D, sc in next st; with C, sc in next 3 sts; with D, sc in next st; with C, sc in next st; with D, sc in next 2 sts; with C, sc in next 4 sts, turn.

Row 20: Ch 1, with C, sc in first st; [with D, sc in next st; with C, sc in next 7 sts] 19 times; with D, sc in next st; with C, sc in next 5 sts, turn.

Row 21: Change to larger hook, drop D to back of work, with C, ch 1, sc in each st across, turn.

Row 22: Ch 1, sc in each st across, turn, fasten off C.

Rows 23 & 24: With D, ch 1, sc in each st across, turn, fasten off D at end of row 24.

STRIPE 7: MERRY CHRISTMAS

Row 1 (RS): With larger hook and RS facing, join A in first st, ch 1, sc in each st across, turn.

Row 2: Ch 1, sc in each st across, turn.

Rows 3 & 4: With B, ch 1, sc in each st across, turn.

Rows 5 & 6: With A, ch 1, sc in each st across, turn.

Rows 7–10: With B, ch 1, sc in each st across, turn.

Row 11: Change to smaller hook, working over color not in use, with B, ch 1, sc in first 3 sts; with A, sc in next 7 sts; [with B, sc in next 4 sts; with A, sc in next st; with B, sc in next 7 sts; with A, sc in next st] 2 times; with B, sc in next 6 sts; with A, sc in next 3 sts; with B, sc in next 6 sts; with A, sc in next 7 sts; with B, sc in next 4 sts; with A, sc in next st; [with B, sc in next 3 sts; with A, sc in next 3 sts] 2 times; with B, sc in next 3 sts; with A, sc in next st; with B, sc in next 7 sts; with A, sc in next st; with B, sc in next 4 sts; with A, sc in next 5 sts; with B, sc in next 10 sts; with A, sc in next 3 sts; with B, sc in next 5 sts; with A, sc in next 3 sts; with B, sc in next 3 sts; with A, sc in next 3 sts; with B, sc in next 2 sts; [with A, sc in next 3 sts; with B, sc in next 3 sts] 2 times; with A, sc in next 6 sts; with B, sc in next 4 sts; with A, sc in next st; with B, sc in next 7 sts; with A, sc in next st; with B, sc in next 3 sts, turn.

Row 12: Ch 1, with B, sc in first 2 sts; with A, sc in next 9 sts; [with B, sc in next 2 sts; with A, sc in next 3 sts; with B, sc in next 5 sts; with A, sc in next 3 sts] 2 times; with B, sc in next 5 sts; with A, sc in next 3 sts; with B, sc in next 5 sts; with A, sc in next 9 sts; with B, sc in next 2 sts; with A, sc in next 3 sts; with B,

sc in next 3 sts; [with A, sc in next 3 sts; with B, sc in next 2 sts] 2 times; with A, sc in next 3 sts; with B, sc in next 5 sts; with A, sc in next 3 sts; with B, sc in next 2 sts; with A, sc in next 7 sts; with B, sc in next 9 sts; with A, sc in next 3 sts; with B, sc in next 6 sts; with A, sc in next 3 sts; with B, sc in next 2 sts; with A, sc in next 3 sts; with B, sc in next 3 sts; [with A, sc in next 3 sts; with B, sc in next 2 sts] 2 times; with A, sc in next 8 sts; with B, sc in next 2 sts; with A, sc in next 3 sts; with B, sc in next 5 sts; with A, sc in next 3 sts; with B, sc in next 2 sts, turn.

Row 13: Ch 1, with B, sc in first 3 sts; with A, sc in next 7 sts; with B, sc in next 4 sts; [with A, sc in next 3 sts; with B, sc in next 3 sts] 2 times; [with A, sc in next 3 sts; with B, sc in next 5 sts] 2 times; with A, sc in next 3 sts; with B, sc in next 6 sts; with A, sc in next 7 sts; with B, sc in next 3 sts; with A, sc in next 3 sts; with B, sc in next 4 sts; with A, sc in next 3 sts; with B, sc in next st; with A, sc in next 3 sts; with B, sc in next 2 sts; with A, sc in next 3 sts; with B, sc in next 5 sts; with A, sc in next 3 sts; with B, sc in next 3 sts; with A, sc in next 7 sts; with B, sc in next 8 sts; with A, sc in next 3 sts; with B, sc in next 7 sts; with A, sc in next 3 sts; with B, sc in next st; with A, sc in next 3 sts; with B, sc in next 4 sts; with A, sc in next 3 sts; with B, sc in next st; with A, sc in next 3 sts; with B, sc in next 3 sts; with A, sc in next 7 sts; with B, sc in next 2 sts; with A, sc in next 3 sts; with B, sc in next 5 sts; with A, sc in next 3 sts; with B, sc in next 2 sts, turn.

Row 14: Ch 1, with B, sc in first 2 sts; with A, sc in next 3 sts; with B, sc in next 10 sts; with A, sc in next 3 sts; with B, sc in next st; with A, sc in next 3 sts; with B, sc in next 4 sts; [with A, sc in next 3 sts; with B, sc in next 5 sts] 3 times; with A, sc in next 3 sts; with B, sc in next 8 sts; with A, sc in next 3 sts; with B, sc in next 5 sts; with A, sc in next 2 sts; with B, sc in next st; with A, sc in next 3 sts; with B, sc in next 2 sts; with A, sc in next 3 sts; with B, sc in next 5 sts; with A, sc in next 3 sts; with B, sc in next 8 sts; with A, sc in next 3 sts; with B, sc in next 7 sts; with A, sc in next 3 sts; with B, sc in next 8 sts; with A, sc in next 2 sts; with B, sc in next st; with A, sc in next 3 sts; with B, sc in next 5 sts; with A, sc in next 2 sts; with B, sc in next st; with A, sc in next 3 sts; with B, sc in next 7 sts; with A, sc in next 3 sts; with B, sc in next 2 sts; with A, sc in next 3 sts; with B, sc in next 5 sts; with A, sc in next 3 sts; with B, sc in next 2 sts, turn.

Row 15: Ch 1, with B, sc in first 3 sts; with A, sc in next 5 sts; with B, sc in next 6 sts; with A, sc in next 9 sts; with B, sc in next 3 sts; with A, sc in next 3 sts; with B, sc in next 2 sts; with A, sc in next st; with B, sc in next 2 sts; with A, sc in next 3 sts; with B, sc in next 5 sts; with A, sc in next 3 sts; with B, sc in next 6 sts; with A, sc in next 5 sts; with B, sc in next 5 sts; with A, sc in next 3 sts; with B, sc in next 4 sts; with A, sc in next 3 sts; with B, sc in next st; with A, sc in next 3 sts; with B, sc in next 2 sts; with A, sc in next 11 sts; with B, sc in next 8 sts; [with A, sc in next 3 sts; with B, sc in next 7 sts] 2 times; [with A, sc in next 3 sts; with B, sc in next st; with A, sc in next 3 sts; with B, sc in next 4 sts] 2 times; with A, sc in next 5 sts; with B, sc in next 3 sts; with A, sc in next 3 sts; with B, sc in next 2 sts; with A, sc in next st; with B, sc in next 2 sts; with A, sc in next 3 sts; with B, sc in next 2 sts, turn.

Row 16: Ch 1, with B, sc in first 4 sts; with A, sc in next 5 sts; with B, sc in next 6 sts; with A, sc in next 7 sts; with B, sc in next 4 sts; [with A, sc in next 3 sts; with B, sc in next st] 2 times; with A, sc in next 3 sts; with B, sc in next 5 sts; with A, sc in next 3 sts; with B, sc in next 7 sts; with A, sc in next 5 sts; with B, sc in next 4 sts; with A, sc in next 3 sts; with B, sc in next 3 sts; with A, sc in next 8 sts; with B, sc in next 2 sts; with A, sc in next 11 sts; with B, sc in next 8 sts; with A, sc in next 3 sts; with B, sc in next 6 sts; with A, sc in next 5 sts; with B, sc in next 5 sts; [with A, sc in next 8 sts; with B, sc in next 3 sts] 2 times; with A, sc in next 6 sts; with B, sc in next 3 sts; [with A, sc in next 3 sts; with B, sc in next st] 2 times; with A, sc in next 3 sts; with B, sc in next 2 sts, turn.

Row 17: Ch 1, with B, sc in first 5 sts; with A, sc in next 5 sts; with B, sc in next 6 sts; with A, sc in next 2 sts; with B, sc in next st; with A, sc in next 2 sts; with B, sc in next 5 sts; [with A, sc in next 3 sts; with B, sc in next st] 2 times; with A, sc in next 3 sts; with B, sc in next 5 sts; with A, sc in next 3 sts; with B, sc in next 8 sts; with A, sc in next 5 sts; with B, sc in next 3 sts; with A, sc in next 3 sts; with B, sc in next 2 sts; with A, sc in next 9 sts; with B, sc in next 2 sts; with A, sc in next 11 sts; with B, sc in next 8 sts; with A, sc in next 3 sts; with B, sc in next 5 sts; with A, sc in next 7 sts; with B, sc in next 3 sts; with A, sc in next 9 sts; with B, sc in next 2 sts; with A, sc in next 9 sts; with B, sc in next 4 sts; with A, sc in next 5 sts; with B, sc in next 3 sts; [with A, sc in next 3 sts; with B, sc in next st] 2 times; with A, sc in next 3 sts; with B, sc in next 2 sts, turn.

Row 18: Ch 1, with B, sc in first 9 sts; with A, sc in next 2 sts; [with B, sc in next 4 sts; with A, sc in next 3 sts; with B, sc in next st; with A, sc in next 3 sts] 2 times; with B, sc in next st; with A, sc in next 3 sts; with B, sc in next 5 sts; with A, sc in next 3 sts; with B, sc in next 12 sts; with A, sc in next 2 sts; with B, sc in next 2 sts; with A, sc in next 3 sts; with B, sc in next 2 sts; with A, sc in next 4 sts; [with B, sc in next 2 sts; with A, sc in next 3 sts] 2 times; with B, sc in next 5 sts; with A, sc in next 3 sts; with B, sc in next 8 sts; with A, sc in next 3 sts; with B, sc in next 4 sts; with A, sc in next 4 sts; with B, sc in next st; [with A, sc in next 4 sts; with B, sc in next 2 sts] 2 times; with A, sc in next 3 sts; with B, sc in next 2 sts; with A, sc in next 4 sts; with B, sc in next 2 sts; with A, sc in next 3 sts; with B, sc in next 7 sts; with A, sc in next 3 sts; with B, sc in next 2 sts; [with A, sc in next 3 sts; with B, sc in next st] 2 times; with A, sc in next 3 sts; with B, sc in next 2 sts, turn.

Row 19: Ch 1, with B, sc in first 3 sts; with A, sc in next 8 sts; with B, sc in next 5 sts; with A, sc in next 5 sts; with B, sc in next 5 sts; with A, sc in next 11 sts; with B, sc in next 2 sts; with A, sc in next 9 sts; with B, sc in next 3 sts; with A, sc in next 8 sts; with B, sc in next 2 sts; with A, sc in next 3 sts; with B, sc in next 2 sts; with A, sc in next 9 sts; with B, sc in next 2 sts; with A, sc in next 3 sts; with B, sc in next 5 sts; with A, sc in next 3 sts; with B, sc in next 3 sts; with A, sc in next 7 sts; with B, sc in next 5 sts; with A, sc in next 4 sts; with B, sc in next st; with A, sc in next 4 sts; [with B, sc in next 2 sts; with A, sc in next 9 sts] 2 times; with B, sc in next 3 sts; with A, sc in next 7 sts; with B, sc in next 2 sts; with A, sc in next 11 sts; with B, sc in next 2 sts, turn.

Row 20: Ch 1, with B, sc in first 2 sts; with A, sc in next 9 sts; with B, sc in next 6 sts; with A, sc in next 3 sts; with B, sc in next 6 sts; with A, sc in next 5 sts; with B, sc in next st; with A, sc in next 5 sts; [with B, sc in next 2 sts; with A, sc in next 9 sts] 2 times; with B, sc in next 2 sts; with A, sc in next 3 sts; with B, sc in next 3 sts; with A, sc in next 8 sts; with B, sc in next 2 sts; with A, sc in next 3 sts; with B, sc in next 5 sts; with A, sc in next 3 sts; with B, sc in next 2 sts; with A, sc in next 7 sts; with B, sc in next 6 sts; [with A, sc in next 3 sts; with B, sc in next 3 sts] 2 times; with A, sc in next 8 sts; with B, sc in next 3 sts; [with A, sc in next 8 sts; with B, sc in next 2 sts] 2 times; with A, sc in next 5 sts; with B, sc in next st; with A, sc in next 5 sts; with B, sc in next 2 sts, turn.

Row 21: Ch 1, with B, sc in first 3 sts; with A, sc in next 7 sts; with B, sc in next 8 sts; with A, sc in next st; with B, sc in next 8 sts; [with A, sc in next 3 sts; with B, sc in next 3 sts] 2 times; with A, sc in next 9 sts; with B, sc in next 3 sts; with A, sc in next 7 sts; with B, sc in next 4 sts; with A, sc in next st; with B, sc in next 5 sts; with A, sc in next 7 sts; with B, sc in next 3 sts; with A, sc in next st; with B, sc in next 7 sts; with A, sc in next st; with B, sc in next 4 sts; with A, sc in next 5 sts; with B, sc in next 6 sts; with A, sc in next 3 sts; with B, sc in next 5 sts; with A, sc in next 3 sts; with B, sc in next 3 sts; with A, sc in next 7 sts; with B, sc in next 4 sts; with A, sc in next 7 sts; with B, sc in next 3 sts; with A, sc in next 6 sts; with B, sc in next 4 sts; [with A, sc in next 3 sts; with B, sc in next 3 sts] 2 times, turn.

Row 22: Change to larger hook, drop A to back of work, with B, ch 1, sc in each st across, turn.

Rows 23–25: Ch 1, sc in each st across, turn.

Rows 26 & 27: With A, ch 1, sc in each st across, turn.

Rows 28 & 29: With B, ch 1, sc in each st across, turn, fasten off B at end of row 29.

Rows 30 & 31: With A, ch 1, sc in each st across, turn, fasten off A at end of row 31.

STRIPE 8: HOUSE

Row 1 (RS): With larger hook and RS facing, join F in first st, ch 1, sc in each st across, turn.

Row 2: Ch 1, sc in each st across, turn.

Rows 3 & 4: With G, ch 1, sc in each st across, turn.

Rows 5 & 6: With F, ch 1, sc in each st across, turn.

Row 7: Change to smaller hook, working over color not in use, with F, ch 1, sc in first 3 sts; [with G, sc in next 9 sts; with F, sc in next 7 sts] 9 times; with G, sc in next 9 sts; with F, sc in next 3 sts, turn.

Rows 8 & 9: Ch 1, with F, sc in first 3 sts; [with G, sc in next 9 sts; with F, sc in next 7 sts] 9 times; with G, sc in next 9 sts; with F, sc in next 3 sts, turn.

Row 10: Ch 1, with F, sc in first 3 sts; [with G, sc in next 2 sts; with F, sc in next 5 sts; with G, sc in next 2 sts; with F, sc in next 7 sts] 9 times; with G, sc in next 2 sts; with F, sc in next 5 sts; with G, sc in next 2 sts; with F, sc in next 3 sts, turn.

Row 11: Ch 1, with F, sc in first 3 sts; [with G, sc in next 2 sts; with F, sc in next st; with G, sc in next st; with F, sc in next st; with G, sc in next st; with F, sc in next st; with G, sc in next 2 sts; with F, sc in next 7 sts] 9 times; with G, sc in next 2 sts; [with F, sc in next st; with G, sc in next st] 2 times; with F, sc in next st; with G, sc in next 2 sts; with F, sc in next 3 sts, turn.

Row 12: Ch 1, with F, sc in first 3 sts; [with G, sc in next 2 sts; with F, sc in next 5 sts; with G, sc in next 2 sts; with F, sc in next 7 sts] 9 times; with G, sc in next 2 sts; with F, sc in next 5 sts; with G, sc in next 2 sts; with F, sc in next 3 sts, turn.

Rows 13 & 14: Ch 1, with F, sc in first 3 sts; [with G, sc in next 9 sts; with F, sc in next 7 sts] 9 times; with G, sc in next 9 sts; with F, sc in next 3 sts, turn.

Row 15: Ch 1, with F, sc in first st; [with G, sc in next 2 sts; with F, sc in next 9 sts; with G, sc in next 2 sts; with F, sc in next 3 sts] 9 times; with G, sc in next 2 sts; with F, sc in next 9 sts; with G, sc in next 2 sts; with F, sc in next st, turn.

Row 16: Ch 1, with F, sc in first st; [with G, sc in next 2 sts; with F, sc in next st; with G, sc in next 7 sts; with F, sc in next st; with G, sc in next 2 sts; with F, sc in next 3 sts] 9 times; with G, sc in next 2 sts; with F, sc in next st; with G, sc in next 7 sts; with F, sc in next st; with G, sc in next 2 sts; with F, sc in next st, turn.

Row 17: Ch 1, with F, sc in first 2 sts; [with G, sc in next 2 sts; with F, sc in next st; with G, sc in next 5 sts; with F, sc in next st; with G, sc in next 2 sts; with F, sc in next 5 sts] 9 times; with G, sc in next 2 sts; with F, sc in next st; with G, sc in next 5 sts; with F, sc in next st; with G, sc in next 2 sts; with F, sc in next 2 sts, turn.

Row 18: Ch 1, with F, sc in first 3 sts; [with G, sc in next 2 sts; with F, sc in next st; with G, sc in next 3 sts; with F, sc in next st; with G, sc in next 2 sts; with F, sc in next 7 sts] 9 times; with G, sc in next 2 sts; with F, sc in next st; with G, sc in next 3 sts; with F, sc in next st; with G, sc in next 2 sts; with F, sc in next 3 sts, turn.

Row 19: Ch 1, with F, sc in first 4 sts; [with G, sc in next 2 sts; with F, sc in next st; with G, sc in next st; with F, sc in next st; with G, sc in next 2 sts; with F, sc in next 9 sts] 9 times; with G, sc in next 2 sts; with F, sc in next st; with G, sc in next st; with F, sc in next st; with G, sc in next 2 sts; with F, sc in next 4 sts, turn.

Row 20: Ch 1, with F, sc in first 3 sts; [with G, sc in next st; with F, sc in next st; with G, sc in next 2 sts; with F, sc in next st; with G, sc in next 2 sts; with F, sc in next 9 sts] 9 times; with G, sc in next st; [with F, sc in next st; with G, sc in next 2 sts] 2 times; with F, sc in next 5 sts, turn.

Row 21: Ch 1, with F, sc in first 3 sts; [with G, sc in next 2 sts; with F, sc in next st; with G, sc in next 3 sts; with F, sc in next 10 sts] 9 times; with G, sc in next 2 sts; with F, sc in next st; with G, sc in next 3 sts; with F, sc in next 6 sts, turn.

Row 22: Ch 1, with F, sc in first 3 sts; [with G, sc in next 2 sts; with F, sc in next 2 sts; with G, sc in next st; with F, sc in next 11 sts] 9 times; with G, sc in next 2 sts; with F, sc in next 2 sts; with G, sc in next st; with F, sc in next 7 sts, turn.

Row 23: Change to larger hook, drop G to back of work, with F, ch 1, sc in each st across, turn.

Row 24: Ch 1, sc in each st across, turn.

Rows 25 & 26: With G, ch 1, sc in each st across, turn, fasten off G at end of row 26.

Rows 27 & 28: With F, ch 1, sc in each st across, turn, fasten off F at end of row 28.

STRIPE 9: SNOWMEN

Row 1 (RS): With larger hook and RS facing, join B in first st, ch 1, sc in each st across, turn.

Row 2: Ch 1, sc in each st across.

Rows 3 & 4: With A, ch 1, sc in each st across, turn.

Row 5: Change to smaller hook, working over color not in use, with A, ch 1, sc in first 8 sts; [with B, sc in next 3 sts; with A, sc in next 11 sts] 10 times; with B, sc in next 3 sts; with A, sc in next 8 sts, turn.

Row 6: Ch 1, with A, sc in first 7 sts; [with B, sc in next 5 sts; with A, sc in next 9 sts] 10 times; with B, sc in next 5 sts; with A, sc in next 7 sts, turn.

Row 7: Ch 1, with A, sc in first 6 sts; [with B, sc in next 3 sts; with A, sc in next st; with B, sc in next 3 sts; with A, sc in next 7 sts] 10 times; with B, sc in next 3 sts; with A, sc in next st; with B, sc in next 3 sts; with A, sc in next 6 sts, turn.

Row 8: Ch 1, with A, sc in first 6 sts; [with B, sc in next 7 sts; with A, sc in next 7 sts] 10 times; with B, sc in next 7 sts; with A, sc in next 6 sts, turn.

Row 9: Ch 1, with A, sc in first 6 sts; [with B, sc in next 3 sts; with A, sc in next st; with B, sc in next 3 sts; with A, sc in next 7 sts] 10 times; with B, sc in next 3 sts; with A, sc in next st; with B, sc in next 3 sts; with A, sc in next 6 sts, turn.

Row 10: Ch 1, [with A, sc in first/next 5 sts; with B, sc in next st; with A, sc in next st; with B, sc in next 5 sts; with A, sc in next st; with B, sc in next st] 11 times; with A, sc in next 5 sts, turn.

Row 11: Ch 1, with A, sc in first 4 sts; [with B, sc in next st; with A, sc in next 3 sts; with B, sc in next 3 sts; with A, sc in next 3 sts; with B, sc in next st; with A, sc in next 3 sts] 10 times; with B, sc in next st; with A, sc in next 3 sts; with B, sc in next 3 sts; with A, sc in next 3 sts; with B, sc in next st; with A, sc in next 4 sts, turn.

Row 12: Ch 1, with A, sc in first 7 sts; [with B, sc in next 2 sts; with A, sc in next st; with B, sc in next 2 sts; with A, sc in next 9 sts] 10 times; with B, sc in next 2 sts; with A, sc in next st; with B, sc in next 2 sts; with A, sc in next 7 sts, turn.

Row 13: Ch 1, with A, sc in first 7 sts; [with B, sc in next st; with A, sc in next st] 2 times; [with B, sc in next st; with A, sc in next 9 sts; with B, sc in next st; with A, sc in next st; with B, sc in next st; with A, sc in next st] 10 times; with B, sc in next st; with A, sc in next 7 sts, turn.

Row 14: Ch 1, with A, sc in first 6 sts; [with B, sc in next 7 sts; with A, sc in next 7 sts] 10 times; with B, sc in next 7 sts; with A, sc in next 6 sts, turn.

Rows 15–17: Ch 1, with A, sc in first 7 sts; [with B, sc in next 5 sts; with A, sc in next 9 sts] 10 times; with B, sc in next 5 sts; with A, sc in next 7 sts, turn.

Row 18: Change to larger hook, drop B to back of work, with A, ch 1, sc in each st across, turn.

Row 19: Ch 1, sc in each st across, turn.

COLOR KEY
- Really red
- Green apple
- Meadow
- Fern green
- Snow white
- Azalea
- Rosewood

Colors in chart have been adjusted from true colors to assist with visibility.

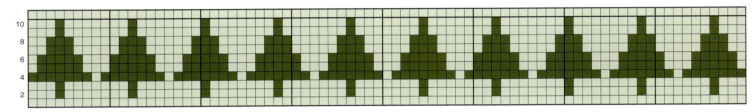

Christmas Dreams Afghan
Trees Chart

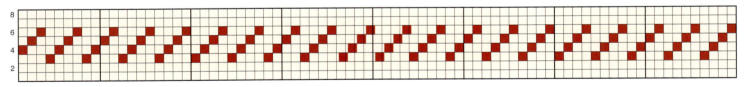

Christmas Dreams Afghan
Candy Cane Chart

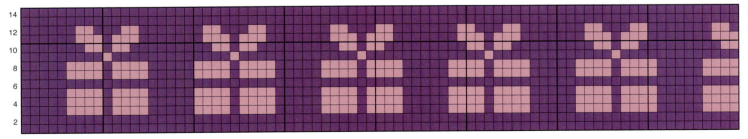

Christmas Dreams Afghan
Gifts Chart

Row 20: With B, ch 1, sc in each st across, turn, fasten off B.

Rows 21 & 22: With A, ch 1, sc in each st across, turn, do not fasten off.

BORDER

Rnd 1 (RS): Ch 1, 3 sc in first sc, **place marker in center st of 3 sc just worked** (see Pattern Notes), sc in next 157 sc, 3 sc in next sc, place marker in center st of 3 sc just worked, rotate to work in row ends on long side of afghan, work 172 sc evenly along edge, rotate to work in unused lps of foundation ch, 3 sc in first foundation ch, place marker in center st of 3 sc just worked, sc in next 157 chs across, 3 sc in last ch, place marker in center st of 3 sc just worked, rotate to work in row ends on 2nd long side of afghan, work 172 sc evenly across, join in first sc. *(670 sc)*

Note: Move markers up each rnd.

Rnd 2: Sl st in next st, ch 1, *3 sc in marked st, sc in each st to next marked st; rep from * 3 times; join in first sc, fasten off A. *(678 sc)*

Rnd 3: Join F in any marked st, (**ch 3**—*see Pattern Notes*, 4 dc) in same st, dc in each sc to next marked st, *5 dc in marked st, dc in each sc to next marked st; rep from * twice, join in top of beg ch-3, fasten off. *(694 dc)*

Rnd 4: Join B in any marked st and work same as rnd 3, fasten off. *(710 dc)*

Rnd 5: Join F in any marked st and work same as rnd 3, fasten off. *(726 dc)*

Rnds 6 & 7: Join A in any marked st and work same as rnd 2, fasten off. *(758 dc)*

FINISHING

Block afghan to measurements. ●

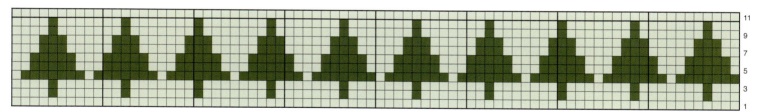

Christmas Dreams Afghan
Trees Chart

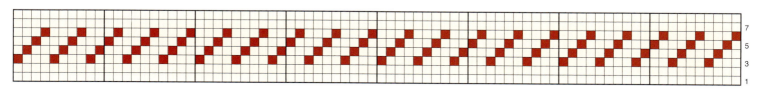

Christmas Dreams Afghan
Candy Cane Chart

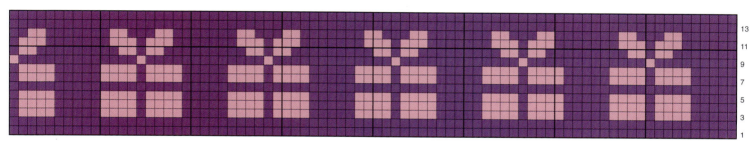

Christmas Dreams Afghan
Gifts Chart

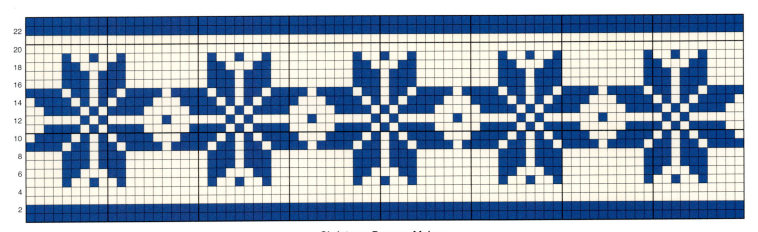

Christmas Dreams Afghan
Snowflakes Chart

COLOR KEY
- Really red
- Green apple
- Meadow
- Fern green
- Snow white
- Azalea
- Rosewood

Colors in chart have been adjusted from true colors to assist with visibility.

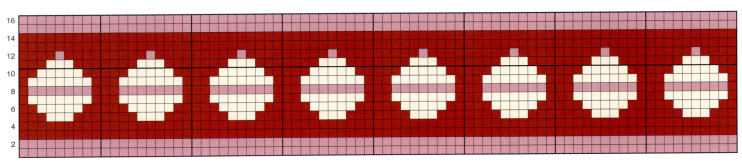

Christmas Dreams Afghan
Ornaments Chart

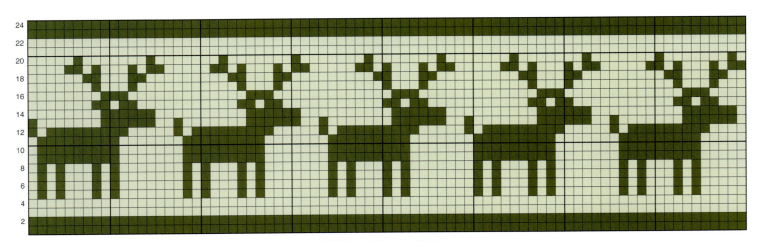

Christmas Dreams Afghan
Reindeer Chart

36

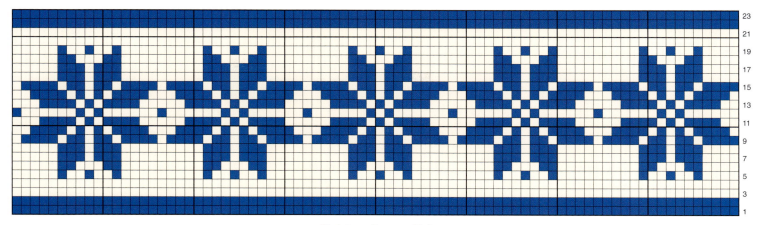
Christmas Dreams Afghan
Snowflakes Chart

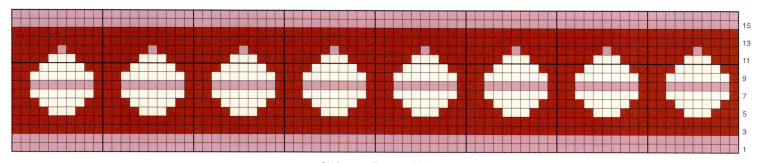
Christmas Dreams Afghan
Ornaments Chart

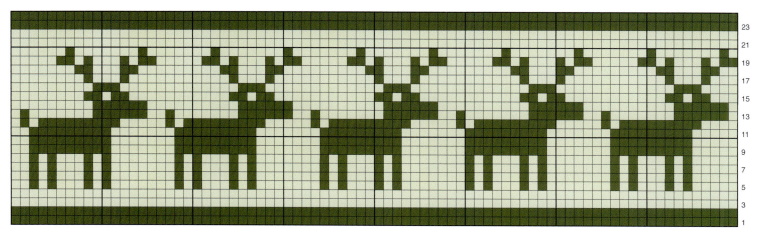
Christmas Dreams Afghan
Reindeer Chart

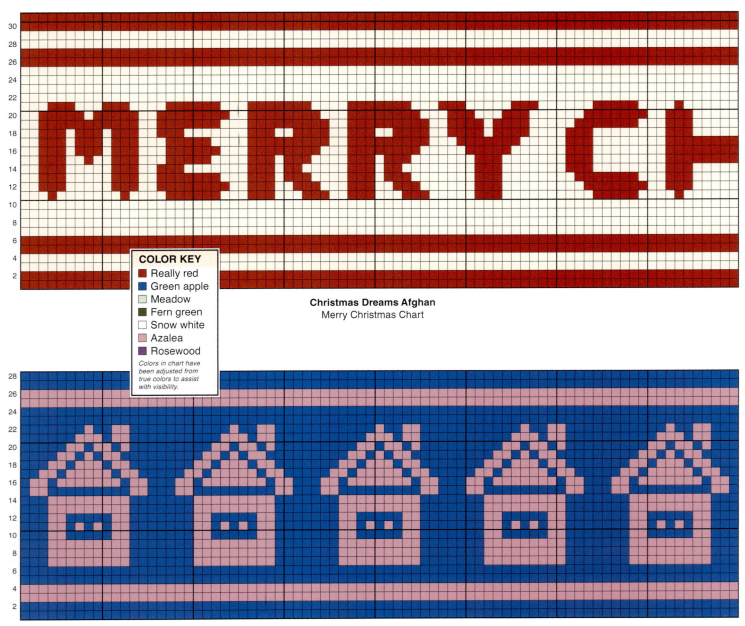

Christmas Dreams Afghan
Merry Christmas Chart

Christmas Dreams Afghan
House Chart

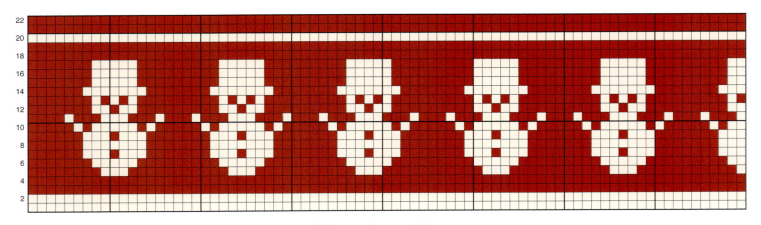

Christmas Dreams Afghan
Snowmen Chart

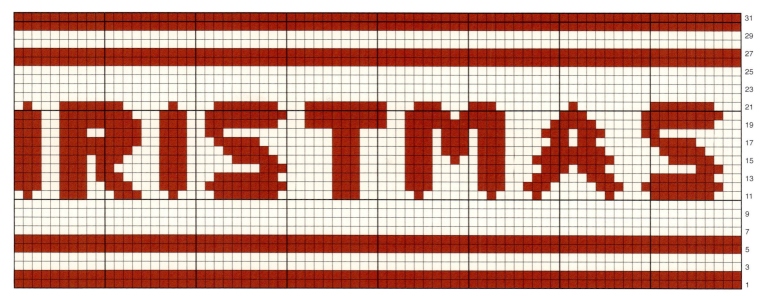

Christmas Dreams Afghan
Merry Christmas Chart

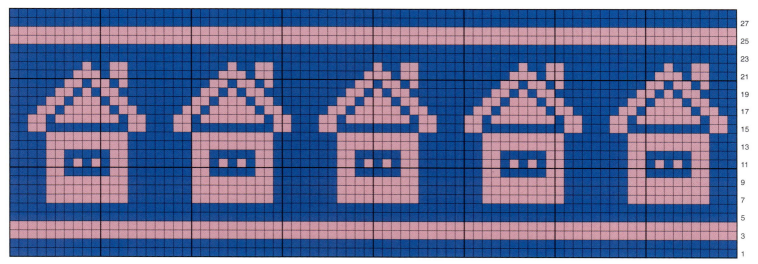

Christmas Dreams Afghan
House Chart

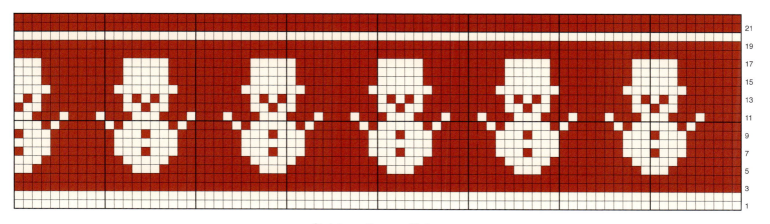

Christmas Dreams Afghan
Snowmen Chart

CLASSIC CHRISTMAS BLOCKS AFGHAN

Design by Jennifer Olivarez

Grab your hot cocoa and get ready to snuggle up under this cozy blanket decorated with beloved symbols of Christmas. Blocks featuring plaid and tree designs are made using tapestry crochet, while the snowflake and poinsettia blocks use post stitches worked in the round to create eye-catching raised designs.

SKILL LEVEL
Intermediate

FINISHED MEASUREMENTS
50 inches wide x 66 inches long

MATERIALS
- Red Heart Super Saver medium (worsted) weight acrylic yarn (7 oz/364 yds/198g per skein):
    3 skeins each #0316 soft white, #0341 light gray and #0319 cherry red
    2 skeins #0389 hunter green
    1 skein each #0631 light sage, #0406 medium thyme and #0360 café latte
- Size G/6/4mm crochet hook or size needed to obtain gauge
- Tapestry needle

GAUGE
16 sc = 4 inches; 16 rows = 4 inches

Snowflake and Poinsettia Blocks: Rnds 1–7 = 6 inches in diameter

PATTERN NOTES
Each block is 8 inches square.

Weave in loose ends as work progresses.

To change color, work last yarn over of last stitch of current color with **new color** (see illustration) for next stitch. Drop color not in use to back of work.

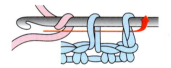

Single Crochet Color Change

Tree Block and Plaid Block are worked with tapestry crochet. Carry unused yarn color along top of stitches of row below, working over strand not in use.

Take care to maintain even tension on carried yarn.

Each square on a colorwork chart represents 1 single crochet. Odd rows are read right to left; even rows are read left to right (reverse for left-handed crocheters).

Chain-3 at beginning of round counts as first double crochet unless otherwise stated.

Join with slip stitch unless otherwise stated.

SPECIAL STITCHES
Single crochet join (sc join): Place slip knot on hook, insert hook in indicated st, yo and pull up a lp, yo and draw through both lps on hook.

Front post double crochet decrease (fpdc dec): Yo, insert hook from front to back to front again around post of indicated st, *yo, pull up a lp, yo and draw through 2 lps*, yo, insert hook from front to back to front again around post of next indicated st, rep from * to * *(3 lps on hook)*, yo, draw through all 3 lps on hook.

Front post half treble crochet (fphtr): Yo 2 times, insert hook from front to back and to front again around post of next indicated st, yo, pull up a lp, yo, pull through 2 lps, yo, pull through 3 lps.

Front post triple treble crochet (fptrtr): Yo 4 times, insert hook from front to back and to front again around post of next indicated st, yo, pull up a lp, [yo, pull through 2 lps] 5 times.

AFGHAN

TREE BLOCK
Make 12.

Row 1 (RS): With soft white, ch 30, sc in **back bar** *(see illustration)* of 2nd ch from hook and in each ch across, turn. *(29 sc)*

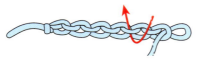

Back Bar of Chain

Row 2: Ch 1, sc in first sc and each sc across, turn.

Row 3: Ch 1, sc in first sc and in next 12 sc; **with café latte** *(see Pattern Notes)*, sc in next 3 sc; with soft white, sc in last 13 sc, turn.

Rows 4–29: Ch 1, **following Tree Chart for color changes** *(see Tree Chart and Pattern Notes)*, sc in first sc and each sc across, turn. Do not turn after last row.

Fasten off medium thyme. Continue with soft white for Tree Block Border.

TREE BLOCK BORDER
Rnd 1 (RS): Rotate to work in ends of rows, ch 1, work 29 sc evenly along row ends, ch 2, rotate to work in opposite side of foundation ch, sc in each ch across, ch 2, rotate to work in ends of rows, work 29 sc evenly along row ends, ch 2, rotate to work across top edge, sc in each sc across, ch 2, **join** *(see Pattern Notes)* in first sc. *(116 sc, 4 ch-2 sps)*

Rnd 2: Ch 1, sc in first sc, [sc in each sc across to next ch-2 sp, (sc, ch 2, sc) in next ch-2 sp] around, join in first sc, fasten off. *(124 sc, 4 ch-2 sps)*

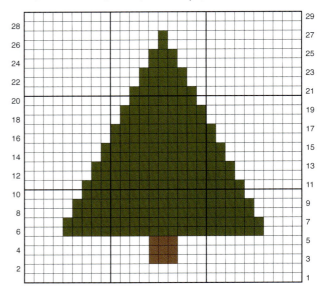

Classic Christmas Blocks Afghan
Tree Chart

PLAID BLOCK
Make 12.

Row 1 (RS): With hunter green, ch 29, sc in back bar of 2nd ch from hook, working in back bar of each ch across, sc in next 3 chs, [with light sage, sc in next 4 chs; with hunter green, sc in next 4 chs] across, turn. *(28 sc)*

Rows 2–28: Ch 1, **following Plaid Chart for color changes** *(see Plaid Chart and Pattern Notes)*, sc in first sc and each sc across, turn.

Fasten off light sage after last row. Continue with hunter green for Plaid Block Border.

PLAID BLOCK BORDER
Note: To make sure all blocks have the same number of edge sts for assembly, you will inc 1 st on the top and bottom edge when working rnd 1 of Border.

Rnd 1 (RS): Ch 1, work 29 sc evenly across top edge, ch 2, rotate to work in ends of rows, work 29 sc evenly along side edge, ch 2, rotate to work in opposite side of foundation ch, work 29 sc evenly across bottom edge, ch 2, rotate to work in ends of rows, work 29 sc evenly along side edge, ch 2, join in first sc. *(116 sc, 4 ch-2 sps)*

Rnd 2: Ch 1, sc in first sc, [sc in each sc across to next ch-2 sp, (sc, ch 2, sc) in next ch-2 sp] around, join in first sc, fasten off. *(124 sc, 4 ch-2 sps)*

Rnd 2: Ch 3, dc in same st, *dc in next dc, **fphtr** *(see Special Stitches)* around same dc**, 2 dc in next dc, rep from * around, ending last rep at **, join in top of beg ch-3. *(18 dc, 6 fphtr)*

Rnd 3: Ch 3, 2 dc in next dc, *dc in next dc, dc in next fphtr, fphtr around same st**, dc in next dc, 2 dc in next dc, rep from * around, ending last rep at **, join in top of beg ch-3. *(30 dc, 6 fphtr)*

Rnd 4: Ch 3, *dc in next dc, 2 dc in next dc, dc in next 2 dc, dc in next fphtr, fphtr around same st**, dc in next dc, rep from * around, ending last rep at **, join in top of beg ch-3. *(42 dc, 6 fphtr)*

Rnd 5: Ch 3, dc in next 6 dc, *dc in next fphtr, fphtr around same st**, dc in next 7 dc, rep from * around, ending last rep at **, join in top of beg ch-3. *(48 dc, 6 fphtr)*

Note: *When working rnd 6 and making a post st 2 rnds below, do not sk a st on rnd 5.*

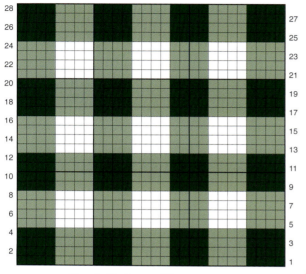

Classic Christmas Blocks Afghan
Plaid Chart

COLOR KEY
- Hunter green
- Light sage
- Soft white

SNOWFLAKE BLOCK
Make 12.

Rnd 1 (RS): With light gray, form a **slip ring** *(see illustration)*, **ch 3** *(see Pattern Notes)*, 11 dc in ring, join in top of beg ch-3. *(12 dc)*

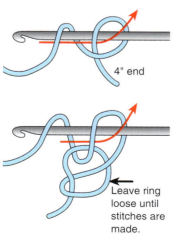

Slip Ring

Rnd 6: Ch 3, dc in next 2 dc, **fptrtr** (see Special Stitches) around last fphtr 2 rnds below, *dc in next 2 dc**, fptrtr around next fphtr 2 rnds below, dc in next 3 dc, fphtr around next fphtr, dc in next 3 dc, fptrtr around same fphtr 2 rnds below as last fptrtr made, rep from * around, ending last rep at **, fptrtr around next fphtr 2 rnds below (same fphtr as first fptrtr made), dc in last 3 dc, fphtr around last fphtr, join in top of beg ch-3. *(48 dc, 12 fptrtr, 6 fphtr)*

Rnd 7: Ch 3, dc in next 9 sts, *dc in next fphtr, fphtr around same st**, dc in next 10 sts, rep from * around, ending last rep at **, join in top of beg ch-3. *(66 dc, 6 fphtr)*

Rnd 8: Ch 3, dc in next dc, *(2 dc, ch 2, 2 dc) in next st, dc in next 2 sts, hdc in next 2 sts, sc in next 9 sts, hdc in next 2 sts**, dc in next 2 sts, rep from * around, ending last rep at **, join in top of beg ch-3. *(36 sc, 16 hdc, 32 dc, 4 ch-2 sps)*

Rnd 9: Ch 3, dc in next 3 sts, *(2 dc, ch 2, 2 dc) in next ch-2 sp, dc in next 4 sts, hdc in next 3 sts, sc in next 7 sts, hdc in next 3 sts**, dc in next 4 sts, rep from * around, ending last rep at **, join in top of beg ch-3. *(28 sc, 24 hdc, 48 dc, 4 ch-2 sps)*

Rnds 10–12: Ch 1, [sc in each st to next ch-2 sp, (sc, ch 2, sc) in next ch-2 sp] 4 times, sc in each rem st, join in first sc. Fasten off after last rnd. *(124 sc, 4 ch-2 sps)*

POINSETTIA BLOCK
Make 12.

Rnd 1 (RS): With cherry red, form a slip ring, ch 3, 15 dc in ring, join in top of beg ch-3. *(16 dc)*

Rnd 2: Ch 3, fphtr around same st as join, *fphtr around next dc, dc in same dc**, dc in next dc, fphtr around same dc, rep from * around, ending last rep at **, join in top of beg ch-3. *(16 dc, 16 fphtr)*

Rnd 3: Ch 3, *dc in next fphtr, fphtr around same st, fphtr around next fphtr**, dc in next 2 dc, rep from * around, ending last rep at **, dc in last dc, join in top of beg ch-3. *(24 dc, 16 fphtr)*

Rnd 4: Ch 3, dc in next dc, *dc in next fphtr, fphtr around same st, fphtr around next fphtr**, dc in next 3 dc, rep from * around, ending last rep at **, dc in last dc, join in top of beg ch-3. *(32 dc, 16 fphtr)*

Rnd 5: Ch 3, dc in next 2 dc, *fphtr around next fphtr, dc in same st, dc in next fphtr, fphtr around same st, sk next dc**, dc in next 3 dc, rep from * around, ending last rep at **, join in top of beg ch-3. *(40 dc, 16 fphtr)*

Rnd 6: Ch 2 *(does not count as a st)*, sk first dc, **dc dec** *(see Stitch Guide)* in next 2 dc, *fphtr around next fphtr, dc in same st, dc in next dc, 2 dc in next dc, dc in next fphtr, fphtr around same st**, dc dec in next 3 dc, rep from * around, ending last rep at **, join in first dc. *(48 dc, 16 fphtr)*

Rnd 7: Ch 3, *derp **fpdc dec** *(see Special Stitches)* around last fphtr and next fphtr, dc in same fphtr as last leg of fpdc dec, dc in next 5 dc, dc in next fphtr**, dc in next dc, rep from * around, ending last rep at **, join in top of beg ch-3. *(64 dc, 8 fpdc)*

Rnd 8: Ch 3, *(2 dc, ch 2, 2 dc) in next st, dc in next 2 dc, hdc in next 2 dc, sc in next 9 dc, hdc in next 2 dc**, dc in next 2 dc, rep from * around, ending last rep at **, dc in last dc, join in top of beg ch-3. *(36 sc, 16 hdc, 32 dc, 4 ch-2 sps)*

Rnd 9: Ch 3, dc in next 2 dc, *(2 dc, ch 2, 2 dc) in next ch-2 sp, dc in next 4 dc, hdc in next 3 sts, sc in next 7 sc, hdc in next 3 sts**, dc in next 4 dc, rep from * around, ending last rep at **, dc in last dc, join in top of beg ch-3. *(28 sc, 24 hdc, 48 dc, 4 ch-2 sps)*

Rnds 10–12: Ch 1, [sc in each st to next ch-2 sp, (sc, ch 2, sc) in next ch-2 sp] 4 times, sc in each rem st, join in first sc. Fasten off after last rnd. *(124 sc, 4 ch-2 sps)*

ASSEMBLY

Block all Blocks to 8 inches square.

With soft white and with RS of each square facing up, using **Assembly Diagram** as a guide, use **invisible seam** *(see illustration)* to sew 8 strips of 6 Blocks each. Then, with an 80-inch length of soft white and with RS of each strip facing up, use invisible seam to sew strips tog.

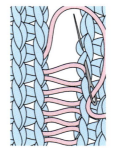

Invisible Seam

BORDER

Rnd 1: Sc join *(see Special Stitches)* hunter green in any st, [sc in each st and ch sp around to next afghan corner ch-2 sp, (sc, ch 2, sc) in corner ch-2 sp] 4 times, sc in each rem st, join in first sc. *(924 sc, 4 ch-2 sps)*

Rnd 2: Ch 3, [dc in each sc across to next ch-2 sp, (2 dc, ch 2, 2 dc) in next ch-2 sp] 4 times, dc in each rem sc, join in top of beg ch-3. *(940 sc, 4 ch-2 sps)*

Rnd 3: Ch 1, sc in first dc, [sc in each dc across to next ch-2 sp, (sc, ch 2, sc) in next ch-2 sp] 4 times, sc in each rem dc, join in first sc. Fasten off. ●

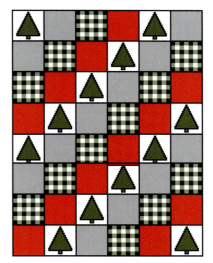

Classic Christmas Blocks Afghan
Assembly Diagram

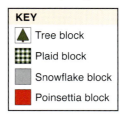

STITCH GUIDE

Need help? 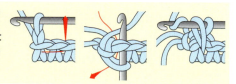 StitchGuide.com • ILLUSTRATED GUIDES • HOW-TO VIDEOS

STITCH ABBREVIATIONS

beg	begin/begins/beginning
bpdc	back post double crochet
bpsc	back post single crochet
bptr	back post treble crochet
CC	contrasting color
ch(s)	chain(s)
ch-	refers to chain or space previously made (i.e., ch-1 space)
ch sp(s)	chain space(s)
cl(s)	cluster(s)
cm	centimeter(s)
dc	double crochet (singular/plural)
dc dec	double crochet 2 or more stitches together, as indicated
dec	decrease/decreases/decreasing
dtr	double treble crochet
ext	extended
fpdc	front post double crochet
fpsc	front post single crochet
fptr	front post treble crochet
g	gram(s)
hdc	half double crochet
hdc dec	half double crochet 2 or more stitches together, as indicated
inc	increase/increases/increasing
lp(s)	loop(s)
MC	main color
mm	millimeter(s)
oz	ounce(s)
pc	popcorn
rem	remain/remains/remaining
rep(s)	repeat(s)
rnd(s)	round(s)
RS	right side(s)
sc	single crochet (singular/plural)
sc dec	single crochet 2 or more stitches together, as indicated
sk	skip/skipped/skipping
sl st(s)	slip stitch(es)
sp(s)	space(s)/spaced
st(s)	stitch(es)
tog	together
tr	treble crochet
trtr	triple treble
WS	wrong side(s)
yd(s)	yard(s)
yo	yarn over

YARN CONVERSION

OUNCES TO GRAMS	GRAMS TO OUNCES
1 .... 28.4	25 .... 7/8
2 .... 56.7	40 .... 1 2/3
3 .... 85.0	50 .... 1 3/4
4 .... 113.4	100 .... 3 1/2

UNITED STATES		UNITED KINGDOM
sl st (slip stitch)	=	sc (single crochet)
sc (single crochet)	=	dc (double crochet)
hdc (half double crochet)	=	htr (half treble crochet)
dc (double crochet)	=	tr (treble crochet)
tr (treble crochet)	=	dtr (double treble crochet)
dtr (double treble crochet)	=	ttr (triple treble crochet)
skip	=	miss

Single crochet decrease (sc dec): (Insert hook, yo, draw lp through) in each of the sts indicated, yo, draw through all lps on hook.

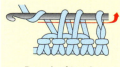

Example of 2-sc dec

Half double crochet decrease (hdc dec): (Yo, insert hook, yo, draw lp through) in each of the sts indicated, yo, draw through all lps on hook.

Example of 2-hdc dec

Reverse single crochet (reverse sc): Ch 1, sk first st, working from left to right, insert hook in next st from front to back, draw up lp on hook, yo and draw through both lps on hook.

Chain (ch): Yo, pull through lp on hook.

Single crochet (sc): Insert hook in st, yo, pull through st, yo, pull through both lps on hook.

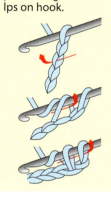

Double crochet (dc): Yo, insert hook in st, yo, pull through st, [yo, pull through 2 lps] twice.

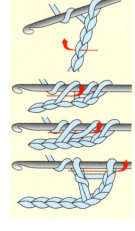

Double crochet decrease (dc dec): (Yo, insert hook, yo, draw lp through, yo, draw through 2 lps on hook) in each of the sts indicated, yo, draw through all lps on hook.

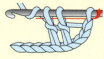

Example of 2-dc dec

Front loop (front lp): Back loop (back lp):

Front post stitch (fp): Back post stitch (bp): When working post st, insert hook from right to left around post of st on previous row.

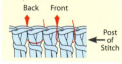

Half double crochet (hdc): Yo, insert hook in st, yo, pull through st, yo, pull through all 3 lps on hook.

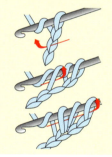

Double treble crochet (dtr): Yo 3 times, insert hook in st, yo, pull through st, [yo, pull through 2 lps] 4 times.

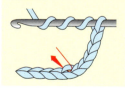

Treble crochet decrease (tr dec): Holding back last lp of each st, tr in each of the sts indicated, yo, pull through all lps on hook.

Example of 2-tr dec

Slip stitch (sl st): Insert hook in st, pull through both lps on hook.

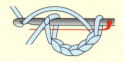

Chain color change (ch color change): Yo with new color, draw through last lp on hook.

Double crochet color change (dc color change): Drop first color, yo with new color, draw through last 2 lps of st.

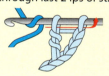

Treble crochet (tr): Yo twice, insert hook in st, yo, pull through st, [yo, pull through 2 lps] 3 times.

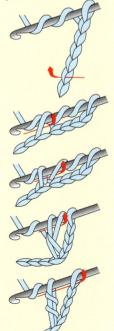

METRIC CONVERSION CHARTS

METRIC CONVERSIONS				
yards	x	.9144	=	meters (m)
yards	x	91.44	=	centimeters (cm)
inches	x	2.54	=	centimeters (cm)
inches	x	25.40	=	millimeters (mm)
inches	x	.0254	=	meters (m)

centimeters	x	.3937	=	inches
meters	x	1.0936	=	yards

INCHES INTO MILLIMETERS & CENTIMETERS (Rounded off slightly)

inches	mm	cm	inches	cm	inches	cm	inches	cm
1/8	3	0.3	5	12.5	21	53.5	38	96.5
1/4	6	0.6	5 1/2	14	22	56	39	99
3/8	10	1	6	15	23	58.5	40	101.5
1/2	13	1.3	7	18	24	61	41	104
5/8	15	1.5	8	20.5	25	63.5	42	106.5
3/4	20	2	9	23	26	66	43	109
7/8	22	2.2	10	25.5	27	68.5	44	112
1	25	2.5	11	28	28	71	45	114.5
1 1/4	32	3.2	12	30.5	29	73.5	46	117
1 1/2	38	3.8	13	33	30	76	47	119.5
1 3/4	45	4.5	14	35.5	31	79	48	122
2	50	5	15	38	32	81.5	49	124.5
2 1/2	65	6.5	16	40.5	33	84	50	127
3	75	7.5	17	43	34	86.5		
3 1/2	90	9	18	46	35	89		
4	100	10	19	48.5	36	91.5		
4 1/2	115	11.5	20	51	37	94		

KNITTING NEEDLES CONVERSION CHART

Canada/U.S.	0	1	2	3	4	5	6	7	8	9	10	10½	11	13	15
Metric (mm)	2	2¼	2¾	3¼	3½	3¾	4	4½	5	5½	6	6½	8	9	10

CROCHET HOOKS CONVERSION CHART

Canada/U.S.	1/B	2/C	3/D	4/E	5/F	6/G	7	8/H	9/I	10/J	10½/K	N
Metric (mm)	2.25	2.75	3.25	3.5	3.75	4	4.5	5	5.5	6	6.5	9.0

Published by Annie's Attic, 306 E. Parr Road, Berne, IN 46711. Printed in USA. Copyright © 2025 Annie's Attic. All rights reserved. This publication may not be reproduced in part or in whole without written permission from the publisher.

Every effort has been made to ensure that the instructions in this publication are complete and accurate. We cannot, however, take responsibility for human error, typographical mistakes or variations in individual work.

ISBN: 979-8-89253-393-5

1 2 3 4 5 6 7 8 9